FUTURE COLLEGE FIELDBOOK

FUTURE COLLEGE FIELDBOOK

Mission, Vision, and Values in Higher Education

Daniel Seymour

Olive Press Publishing

ISBN: 1519401760
ISBN 13: 9781519401762
Library of Congress Control Number: 2015919391
CreateSpace Independent Publishing Platform
North Charleston, South Carolina

Contents

Introduction

There is a pithy exchange between Alice and the Cat in Lewis Carroll's classic book *Alice in Wonderland* (1865) that goes:

"Alice: Would you tell me, please, which way I ought to go from here?
The Cat: That depends a good deal on where you want to get to.
Alice: I don't much care where.
The Cat: Then it doesn't much matter which way you go."

Alice's trip down the rabbit hole into a fantasy world filled with anthropomorphic creatures—White Rabbit, Knave of Hearts, and the Duchess—remains one of the best examples of the genre known as "literary nonsense." The humorous effect that is created by Carroll's use of this technique allowed him to explore very serious topics. Precisely 150 years later, the moral of that little girl's chat with a cat—that is, "If you don't know where you are going, any road will take you there"—has profound meaning for higher education.

How did we get here? How is it that a mid-19th century, talking Cheshire cat could provide useful advice to modern-day colleges and universities?

The problem begins with a gap. Institutions of higher education in this country have been remarkably successful since the time of the founding of Harvard College in 1636. Over the intervening decades and centuries, the U.S. has fought wars, gone through devastating natural disasters, endured economic crises, and suffered many other tragic events. Still, today our higher education system is large, diverse, and respected around the world. The *Times Higher Education* world university rankings placed 15 U.S. institutions—public and private—in the top 20 for 2014-15. Our smaller, liberal arts colleges allow students to develop a broad range of intellectual capacities while our community college model is universally seen as a vehicle to expand social and economic mobility.

One of the key reasons for this enduring success involves organizational structure. Colleges and universities are expert "pigeonholers." We start with silos—instruction, student services, and business. We have our divisions and departments. We reward specialization and resist being lumped together because such "lumping" doesn't fully recognize our perceived specialness. We slice and dice. We divide and conquer. The result is the kind of loosely-coupling described by Karl Weick in his classic 1976 article, "Educational Organizations as Loosely Coupled Systems." In such a system, or organizational structure, each of the components operates with little or no knowledge or control from other components. They have less interdependency, less coordination, and less information flow.

Such systems do well historically in stable environments. Any individual external event will be dealt with by the appropriate unit. Any change that is needed will be tolerated because it will be incremental. The primacy of the pigeonholes will be maintained.

But what happens when the environment within which the organization operates—political economic, social, and technological—becomes hyper-active? What happens when these elements begin to interact in powerful ways that are fundamentally disruptive to the kind of incrementalism experienced in the past? Such high velocity environments require a coordinated response in order to ensure future viability. Or to quote Jack Welch, the ex-CEO of General Electric:

"When the rate of change outside an organization exceeds the rate of change inside, the end is in sight."

The emerging gap, then, comes from the difference between the capabilities associated with loose coupling in colleges and universities and the nature of the environment within which we are now operating. At a time when we need more interdependence, more coordination, and more information flow, we seem to be constrained by a system and structure that continues to venerate the parts over the whole.

Just as nature abhors a vacuum, the gap just described is unsustainable. It will be filled. If we are unclear when describing why we exist, where we are going, and what we value, then someone else will be happy to provide that clarity for us. Indeed, some large portion of the new era of accountability is the result of this fundamental abdication of our responsibility to create of our own futures—or *Future College*.

The fact is, if we don't know where we are going, others will be happy to tell us where to go.

Structure of Book

While the main emphasis of this book centers on a critical examination of 141 colleges and universities, an initial chapter describes a series of core concepts. These concepts provide a set of lenses through which the primary research results can be interpreted. As such, they allow readers to synthesize individual results that occur across both the institutional types and the direction-setting elements being studied—mission, vision, and values. It is an exercise in pattern recognition and so the language in this first chapter is repeated throughout the remainder of the book, reinforcing key themes that can be translated into strategic choices.

The Core Concepts chapter is followed by General Findings. While most of the analyses are chapter specific, there are a few findings that are universal and cut across all of our colleges and universities. Those findings are presented here.

❖ ❖ ❖

The primary research conducted for the book is enumerated in the next three foundational chapters. Mission, vision, and values are the traditional elements associated with what an institution is all about—its purpose, its future, and what it holds dear. Each of these chapters begins with a short background that provides both context and perspective. For this reason, a broad view is taken that includes organizations other than colleges and universities. The data are then analyzed by institutional types because of the expectation that there could be important differences between and among them. Addressing such differences helps to improve the usefulness of the findings. The specific value of primary research is evident in these chapters because of the patterns revealed and the illustrations provided.

Importantly, each of these three principal chapters concludes with a "Questions to Ask" section that is both detailed and comprehensive. The focus shifts from the institutions studied throughout the chapters to the reader's own institution at the end of these chapters.

The final chapter, Promising Practices, enumerates a series of actions that institutions should consider when asking the question: *Which way do we go?* It is clear that if we don't ask and answer this particular question, others will do it for us. As noted, this defines the era of accountability. It is reactive. It is negative. There is nothing positive or generative about someone else holding us accountable. Indeed, externally-driven accountability initiatives all flow from the same source: the abdication of our responsibility. These, then, are a series of prescriptions that are appropriate across institutional types and that seek to empower colleges and universities to create their own futures.

While it is true that, "If you *don't know* where you are going, any road will take you there," it also follows that, "If you *do know* where you are going, you still must choose a road and travel it."

A destination is just a dream without a plan to get there.

Who and How

There are many different types of institutions in American higher education. This book focuses on three of those types through a stratified sampling process. The Carnegie Classification of Institutions of Higher Education identify them as follows:

Baccalaureate Colleges (Arts and Sciences)
Research Universities (Very High Research Activity)
Master's Colleges and Universities (Larger Programs)

Carnegie lists 271 institutions in the Baccalaureate Colleges (Arts and Sciences) classification. These are undergraduate teaching institutions that tend to develop general intellectual capacities rather than vocational skills. Most of them, such as Grinnell College and Pomona College, are private with only a few public institutions. They (see Appendix A) are included because they represent such a rich tradition in American higher education and because they remain an important choice for many students who want the experience these largely residential institutions provide.

The next grouping is Research Universities (Very High Research Activity) that contains a total of 108 institutions. Public institutions such as Purdue University and Georgia Tech University fall into this category as do such privates as Carnegies Mellon University and the University of Southern California. They, of course, are large institutions, with large numbers of students, and have missions that involve a significant focus on research and therefore provide a very different experience for their students and stakeholders. The institutions included in this examination are also enumerated in Appendix A.

There are a total of 413 Master's College and Universities (Larger Programs) in this final Carnegie Classification and includes such public institutions as Marshall University and Texas State University and such privates as Chapman University and Emerson University. These types of institutions (see Appendix A) are included because there are so many and they provide such a broad range of educational programs and services to many students in this country.

And which institutions are not included in the sample? The obvious classification that is not included is Associate degree or two-year colleges. They have both unique missions and educate almost half of all post-secondary students in this country. A critical examination of 224 community colleges has been conducted and published in *Noble Ambitions: Mission, Vision, and Values in American Community Colleges* (2013). It provides a rigorous analysis of the institutions, copious illustrations, and enumerates a set of specific recommendations for community colleges to achieve their noble ambitions.

The other major grouping not included is Carnegie's Special Focus institutions: faith-related institutions, tribal colleges, schools of art, music, and design, military schools, women's colleges, and historically black universities. While each of these institutions plays a role in providing higher education services, by definition they have a narrow focus and specialized missions and, as such, any generalizations would be severely limited.

Within the institutions studied, this is a book to be used by groups of people as opposed to individuals. Throughout the Core Concepts and Promising Practices chapters, and in other areas as well, you will hear the language of inclusion—e.g., a compelling "shared" vision, a "collective" ambition. The questions associated with mission (Why do we exist?), vision (What do we want to create?), and values (What do we believe?) are purposeful in the use of the first-person, plural personal pronoun . . . "we."

Moving an organization from Point A to Point B is a team sport. It cannot be successfully accomplished by reactions to external pressures or events, accountability-driven or otherwise.

For example, earthquakes will happen. Floods and fire occur. While we cannot control if or when such things happen, we can anticipate them and plan accordingly. Indeed, when earthquakes hit, some buildings collapse while others remain intact. The ones that do well are "designed" to be successful. That requires groups of people working together to build in that capacity. Again, individuals at any level of the institution, no matter how well-intentioned or visionary in nature, cannot build capacity.

It takes a team.

❖ ❖ ❖

Which brings us to a second issue—How to use the book. First, this book is referred to as a "fieldbook." Peter Senge's national bestseller, *The Fifth Discipline* (1990), introduced the theory of learning organizations to many business managers (and others who saw the value of a systems approach in their organizations). But the nagging question for many readers was, "What should we do on Monday morning?" And so Senge, and a team of coauthors, published a follow-up book, *The Fifth Discipline Fieldbook* (1994), which was described as an "intensely pragmatic guide." In a similar fashion, this book is decidedly not an academic exercise—a polite, solitary read on an occasional weekend.

***Future College Fieldbook* is a critical examination loaded with examples, questions, and promising practices. Its measure of effectiveness is being dog-eared and highlighted with notes in the margins—also, an intensely pragmatic guide.**

Next, the "how" is closely related to the previous question of "who." Things tend to stick in any organization when they are perceived to be part of the normal rhythm and flow. It is the outliers that are seen as different—*not part of how we do things around here*—that get rejected or marginalized over time.

This presents a problem.

While the act of creating your college's future can and should be an engaging, energizing exercise for an institution, it is also likely to be a departure from the status quo which, in turn, will undoubtedly scare a lot of people.

The best way to proceed is to rely heavily on the shared governance principles of informed and inclusive decision-making. In particular, there are two substantive exercises that fill the criteria of being both part of the rhythm of higher education and broadly inclusive: accreditation and strategic planning.

Every regional accrediting agency has language in their standards or criteria that requires institutions to describe their missions and then detail how they are going to implement suitable strategies, assess their effectiveness, and engage in a process of continuous improvement. While accreditors typically have six- to ten-year cycles, the specific planning efforts at individual institutions are usually shorter (three to five) and often detail strategies and tactics, implementation plans, and key performance indicators that usually begin with a description of mission, vision, and values.

In both cases, workshops are held and teams formed. The real challenge in these settings is that such collaborative efforts often turn inward. They become brainstorming sessions in which individuals are encouraged to share their ideas based upon their personal beliefs. Such idea-sharing initiatives, by themselves, limit the institution's choices. That is because the conversations usually start with a series of, "I think we should . . .," and then go from there. While being passionate and sincere, the fact remains that these exchanges are devoid of any robust criteria associated with promising or best practices. They are simply individual opinions based upon personal experiences and biases.

This book makes the case for doing much more. It suggests that colleges and universities embrace their responsibility to broaden the dialogue to include a clear understanding of the terms involved and their purposes. The "Questions to Ask" sections at the end of the mission, vision, and values chapters as well as the final Promising Practices chapter are specifically included to promote productive conversations.

It is also clear that the mission, vision, and values should work together to create a powerful dynamic that is both distinctive and drives strategic choices.

In other words, your "future college" is far too important a topic in a high velocity environment to leave to a series of conversations among colleagues and stakeholders. There needs to be much greater rigor in the dialogue, there needs to be more and better information available in the analyses.

Like Alice, your institution needs to get a lot more serious in deciding which way to go.

❖ ❖ ❖

1

Core Concepts

Before diving into the details of your college's future, it is useful to offer a few wide-angle observations. Indeed, this chapter offers a series of ideas or concepts that allow readers to frame the conversation moving forward. Each of the content chapters on mission, vision, and values is based upon a critical examination of dozens of institutions within each category. The emphasis is on granularity—looking at individual words being used and the phrasing that is developed. Relying upon such individual observations to reach general conclusions is, of course, the definition of inductive reasoning.

This chapter allows us to apply some deductive reasoning as well. By beginning with some general observations (or hypotheses), it is possible to examine individual data points with some initial constructs in mind. Using such an approach can be illuminating and allow themes to emerge in more coherent ways. In our case, it also allows the use of specific language in the primary research chapters without stopping to define terms or explain the origin of the conclusions being made.

There are four framing concepts: collective ambition, structural tension, emotional contagion, and constancy of purpose. Mission, vision, and values (MVVs) are too often treated as stand-alone elements. The benefits associated with each of these core concepts extend the impact of MVVs in meaningful ways:

1. Collective ambition: MVV as part of a larger system of relationships.
2. Structural tension: MVV as a way to catalyze action based upon the discrepancy between a desired state and an actual state.

3. Emotional contagion: MVV as a means to create positivity such that success becomes the platform for even greater successes.
4. Constancy of purpose: MVV as a way to shift from the problems of today to the promises of tomorrow.

Collective Ambition

Mission, vision, and values are usually described as separate statements in organizations. This makes a lot of sense since the elements are really the answers to separate questions: The answer to the question, "Why do we exist?" is a mission statement; the answer to the question, "What do we want to create?," is the vision statement; and the answer to the question, "What do we believe?," is a statement of values. But while these are powerful concepts individually, they can have even greater influence when seen in a larger context with defined connections.

This interconnectedness has been described by Doulas Ready and Emily Truelove in a *Harvard Business Review* (2011) article entitled, "The Power of Collective Ambition." The authors studied companies across industries that managed to defy conventional logic and thrive during the recent Great Recession. The model that resulted is expressed in what they call *collective ambition*—"a summary of how leaders and employees think about why they exist, what they hope to accomplish, how they will collaborate to achieve their ambition, and how their brand promise aligns with their core values."

So what elements does an organization's collective ambition comprise? There are seven:

---

1. **Purpose: your organization's reason for being; the core mission of the enterprise.**
2. **Vision: the position or status your company aspires to achieve within a certain time frame.**

3. **Targets and milestones: the metrics you use to assess progress toward your vision.**
4. **Strategic and operational priorities: the actions you do or do not take in pursuit of your vision.**
5. **Brand promise: the commitments you make to stakeholders (customers, communities, investors, employees, regulators, and partners) concerning the experience your organization will provide.**
6. **Core values: the guiding principles that dictate what you stand for as an organization, in good times and bad.**
7. **Leader behaviors: how leaders act on a daily basis as they seek to implement the organization's vision and strategic priorities, strive to fulfill the brand promise, and live up to the values.**

Further, the authors use a design of concentric circles to represent collective ambition. They think of it as a compass with purpose at the center. The outermost ring contains the leader behaviors that enable progress. Vision, brand promise, strategic and operational priorities, and values lie in between, along with the targets and milestones that measure progress.

The importance of this model for this book is that it focuses on relationships. For example, a college or university's mission statement is a basic requirement for regional accreditation. It needs to be the result of an inclusive process and it needs to be printed in the catalogue. But a mission statement asks and answers only a single question about purpose. It has, by itself, a very limited ability to engage stakeholders and to provide the kind of aspirational language associated with an organization that is on the move. Moreover, a higher education mission statement is probably incapable of catalyzing the kind of action necessary to thrive in a high velocity environment.

So, while the pieces are important, this concept suggests that the interactions—*the collective*—is what makes ambitions robust and forceful. It turns a static list of isolated ideas into a dynamic construct that is capable of producing momentum in your college or university.

Structural Tension

One way in which colleges and universities are unique from other organizations is accreditation. And all regional accrediting agencies require (as we will examine in detail in the next chapter) that the institution must have a mission statement. For example, the North Central Association's Higher Learning Commission very first criterion states that, "The institution's mission is clear and articulated publicly; it guides the institution's operations." But there is nothing mandated about having a vision statement or a described set of values.

So, why are they important as part of a collective ambition?

Missions, visions, and values are important not simply for what they say but, importantly, for what they can do. And what they can do is create a bias for action. One of the best ways to both understand and visualize this dynamic is through a simple model developed by Robert Fritz in *The Path of Least Resistance for Managers* (1999). In his First Law of Organizational Structure, Fritz states that "organizations either oscillate or advance." Oscillation is really the act of responding to disturbances in the environment and the result is usually a series of fire-fighting exercises. It is literally back-and-forth, back-and-forth, and as soon as one problem is solved another crisis breaks out. In contrast, structural advancement is all about forward movement and is described by Fritz in the following way:

> **"There is one major telltale sign that an organization is advancing: its achievements are a platform for further achievements. For an organization that is advancing, everything counts; even those things that don't work are transformed into significant learning that eventually leads to success."**

But exactly how does this happen? The secret to success is structural tension. The center portion of the model shows an "actual state" and a "desired state." When there is a difference between these two states the result is a "discrepancy." While this may sound like a bad thing, the fact is when a discrepancy doesn't exist the tendency is for the organization and the individuals to become a bit too comfortable. They tend to pull back, become less engaged, and therefore become more reactive to their environment. But when a discrepancy does exist, it leads to "structural tension" or a type of non-equilibrium.

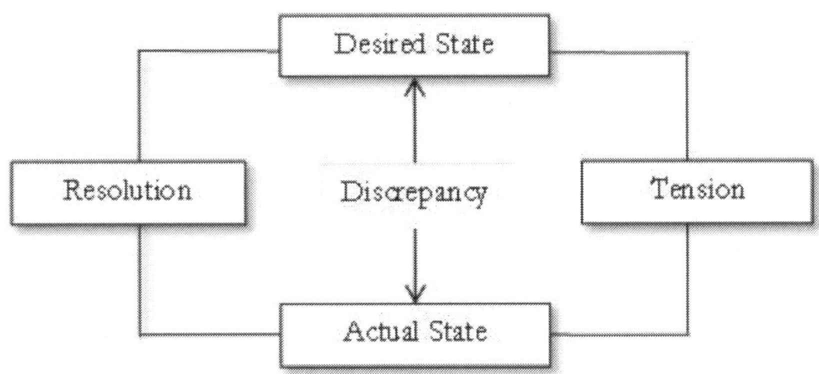

"Resolution," on the opposite side of the model, is really the process of the structure attempting to restore equilibrium. Good enough is simply not good enough. The comfortableness of the status quo is replaced by the tension in knowing that your isntitution can, and must, do better.

Emotional Contagion

Why does structural tension—a difference between a desired state and an actual state—create a bias for action? That is because it creates a positive, uplifting force for change. "Lift" is an individual idea or state of mind that has organizational implications. It is defined as, "a psychological state in which a person is purpose-centered, internally directed, other-focused, and externally open" by Ryan and Robert Quinn in their 2009 book, *Lift: Becoming a Positive Force in Any Situation.* The book jacket summarizes the concept in metaphorical terms:

"Just as the Wright Brothers combined science and practice to achieve the dream of flight, Ryan and Robert Quinn combine research and experience to demonstrate how we can elevate ourselves and the

situations and the people around us to greater heights of integrity, openness, and achievement—to achieve the psychological equivalent of aerodynamic lift."

Underlying the notion of "lift" is appreciating the difference between being comfort-centered and being purpose-centered. Most of the time, most of the people are focused on creating comfort in their lives. The day-to-day, the familiar, is reassuring. We don't like surprises or conditions that could cause stress. The situations that we seek out are predictable, like the plotlines of our favorite sitcoms on television. When challenges disrupt the calm and quiet of the status quo we shift quickly into a problem solving mode. We are intent on making the difficulties disappear so that we can return to a more pastoral existence.

A purpose-centered life stands in stark contrast to the scenario described above. As the Quinn brothers' state:

"The question 'What result do I want to create?' energizes people because it leads them to pursue results that are self-determined ("What do I want . . .') and that challenge them in positive ways (' . . .to create?'). Creating implies doing something positive, difficult, and new rather than relying on existing expectations about what can and cannot be done. Energy alone, however, is insufficient. People need to know how and where to exert that energy, which is why this question also focuses on creating results. Self-chosen, challenging, positive goals give people results to focus on as well as energy for pursuing those results."

Now, here is the key. A variety of disciplines—social and developmental psychology, cultural psychology, history, and so on—have developed compelling evidence to suggest that various moods are communicated from one or more people to others. So, as we have established, "lift" is not related to being comfortable. It is a function of striving. It is being positive about what a bold future holds rather than rallying to defend what we have already achieved. We thrive when we stop reacting to the problems and start developing the capability to create our own futures.

As individuals, we lift ourselves when we have new ideas, new directions, and new energy. But as organizations, the impact of individuals lifting each other creates "emotional contagion" that is palpable—success is expected and becomes the platform for even greater successes. The result for us is colleges and universities that experience virtuous cycles. Failures are interpreted as mere bumps in the road while successes are expected and build into winning streaks.

Striving leads to thriving as structural tension produces a positive energy that is contagious.

Constancy of Purpose

The final core concept has a storied genesis. W. Edwards Deming was an engineer who worked in an area known as statistical process control in post-WW2 Japan. He emphasized the idea that quality was a function of not only statistical controls but of empowering individuals. As such, he became increasingly influential as a management thinker.

In addition to being a university professor and prolific consultant to many major corporations, he also wrote a now-famous book in 1982—*Out of the Crisis*. Deming offered a theory of management based on his famous "14 Points for Management." These key principles for management range from the practical to the philosophical with all of them intended to be transformative in nature. For example:

- Cease dependence on inspection to achieve quality. Eliminate the need for inspection on a mass basis by building quality into the product in the first place.
- Break down barriers between departments. People in research, design, sales, and production must work as a team, to foresee problems of production and in use that may be encountered with the product or service.

- Improve constantly and forever the system of production and service, to improve quality and productivity, and thus constantly decrease costs.

It is easy to see why these, and the other, principles developed a broader appeal beyond business and manufacturing. The idea of building quality into the learning and teaching process—rather than just using a final exam to rank and sort students—is widely accepted. Certainly the understanding that students don't see "student services" and "academic affairs" as separate entities (and barriers) is important to student success and completion. And continuous improvement is a concept that accrediting agencies have embraced as part of a larger model of institutional effectiveness.

But the principle "point" is the one that truly informs this critical examination of mission, vision, and values in colleges and universities:

"Create constancy of purpose toward improvement of product and service, with the aim to become competitive and to stay in business, and to provide jobs."

Management has two fundamental concerns: one deals with running the business on a day-to-day basis; the other deals with the future of the business. Management's failure to plan for the future, according to Deming, brings about loss of market, which brings about loss of jobs. As such, management should not be judged just by a quarterly dividend, but by innovative plans to stay in business, protect investment, ensure future dividends, and provide more jobs through improving products and services.

Colleges and universities can easily get caught up in the rhythm of the enterprise—admitting prospective students, communicating a class schedule, enrolling students in classes, teaching those classes, and giving grades: rinse and repeat. In the spring we don our regalia and commence; in the fall we come together again in convocation to continue running the business—and all of its daily challenges. We can, and often are, consumed with responding to immediate events. We identify the problem, generate a few options, and implement a solution. We fight fires.

But the problems of the future require constancy of purpose and dedication to improvement not just being decisive about the crisis *du jour*. Purpose is "an intent, a goal, a vision of some future desired state" while "constancy involves being faithful or devoted to a cause." Together, they suggest that a significant portion of an organization's time should be devoted to peering over the horizon, identifying a compelling shared vision, and then being devotional about plans to achieve those aspirations.

❖ ❖ ❖

Colleges and universities that have discussions about their purpose and their vision for tomorrow often tend to start with a deep dive into their own surroundings. Meetings in which values or beliefs are discussed get very personal, very quickly. Also, when these discussions are part of accreditation or a strategic planning effort the tendency is to have senior leaders involved, ones who have been part of the institution for a long time—so, smart people, senior people, passionate people.

Under such conditions the tendency is for individual after individual to state their personal opinions. Again, that is what smart people usually do. They are decisive. They want to make decisions and rely on their extensive experience.

This chapter suggests something different: withhold judgment. There is no need to be decisive. There is a need to engage in constructive dialogue and productive conversations. Due diligence is what is important, not the perceived need of individuals to demonstrate their intelligence or to exercise their authority.

There should be no rush. Why not take the time to do a little context setting? Rather than ratcheting down the microscope and focusing on individual words and phrasing that are solely informed from personal experience, the better approach is to use a telescope to scan the horizon for available framing concepts.

The idea that mission, vision, and values—as well as other elements—can combine to form a *collective ambition* is critical to this reflective practice. It follows that a collective ambition is organized in such a way as to create discrepancy between a desired state and an actual state—*structural tension*. That tension, in turn, creates the conditions under which positivity flourishes and the institution gains traction. This *emotional contagion* helps to overcome the comfort-driven inertia that dominates many institutional cultures. The result is a focus on the future that shifts the paradigm from fighting the problems of today to seeking out the opportunities of tomorrow. We become purpose driven. And if we stick to that future focus, that *constancy of purpose*, your institution will have the capacity to thrive even in challenging times.

❖ ❖ ❖

2

General Findings

The idea behind a volume with "Fieldbook" in the title is to be entirely clear about its use. The list of higher education books can be divided into the "To's" and the "For's." The trade books specialize in describing what the authors want to do "to" higher education. They describe their prescriptions about containing the cost of college, disrupting the complacency of college, and arguing for or against the liberal traditions of college. They use soaring rhetoric and data-driven charts to build their cases. All of them—journalists, TV hosts, columnists, pundits, and ex-professors—have opinions that are screaming to be heard.

The manuscripts that are "for" higher education tend to be lower in volume and written by college professors and administrators. Many are narrow and focused on our need to advance a discipline or sub-specialty. Others are extremely broad and consist of policy manifestos that advocate for sweeping changes.

And then there are the few.

These are the books that are intended to support faculty, staff, and administrators who need to make decisions every day that directly impact the future of their colleges and universities. These individuals do not have the time to debate national policy issues and do not have the luxury of extended examinations of disciplinary questions. With the headwinds we are facing—costs, outcomes, accountability—they need to demonstrate their responsibility and make informed choices about which way to go.

A critical examination of a large number of institutions' mission, vision, and values against specific sets of evaluative criteria is needed—an intensely pragmatic guide.

As described in the Introduction, a stratified sample was employed because of the belief that different institutional types within the population of colleges and universities might vary—that is, it is reasonable to think that the issues and challenges associated with describing a future would be different for a small, private liberal arts college than a large, public research universities. Again, the Carnegie Classifications of Institutions of Higher Education categories that were explored were: Baccalaureate Colleges (Arts and Sciences); Research Universities (Very High Research Activity); and Master's Colleges and Universities (Larger Programs).

But in conducting the critical examination across these three different institutional types it also became obvious there were general findings that emerged. This chapter identifies four:

1. The Homepage: The critical examination involved first going to an institution's homepage in order to find the mission, vision, and value statements. This follows because in the new digital age an institution's electronic presence provides the broadest exposure to future students, current students, alums, community members, employees, and every other possible stakeholder group. And so, the question is, "What, if anything, does an institution's homepage reveal about its future?"
2. About _______: The second general finding emerged from the specific search used to find the institution's mission, vision, and values. The question is "Where is the future described?" The tab "About ________," which is usually a part of the horizontal navigation bar, is the location of most of this information.
3. Connecting the Dots: Next, there is the issue of the institution's collective ambition and how the pieces fit together into a coherent whole. "Connecting the dots" involves finding the other elements (e.g., strategic plan) associated with this coherency and establishing if and how they are linked together.
4. Currency: Finally, there is the issue of currency or "the state of being current or up-to-date." This finding is, in many ways, a test of an institution's conviction or constancy of purpose by asking, "Are we making focused progress on our need to create our own future?"

The Homepage

This critical examination begins with an institution's homepage, which at many institutions get more than 1 million unique visits each month. Today's higher education homepages are branding tools. Whether it is a liberal arts college in Iowa or a research university in New York, the principle idea is to grab your attention in a few short seconds and then use various techniques to reinforce an image of the institution.

One way that many now do this is by large tiles. "Events" or "In the News" tiles suggest that the institution is a current and relevant brand. Another common tile is "Rankings" that tout any ranking from any source as proof of the institution's national reputation. Another consistent design element is "Alumni," especially famous ones. Brandeis University has its "Notable Alumni" and begins, "Brandeis counts among its graduates Pulitzer Prize winners, Emmy Award winners, best-selling authors — even a Nobel laureate. But it doesn't stop there. Brandeis graduates occupy leadership roles in virtually every walk of life. Here are just a few." The list is then divided into such categories as Activism and Public Service, Arts and Entertainment, Authors, Business and Industry, Education, Government and Politics, Journalism and Media, Science and Mathematics, and Sports.

The implication is that if you come to College X you too will become a successful alum and add to the reputation of the institution.

Another commonality is the use of infographics. These are simply large numbers used to command attention and reinforce the brand. Bucknell University's homepage sends a message:

- 0% Number of classes taught by grad students
- 9:1 Our student-faculty ratio
- 50/60 More than 50 majors and 65 minors
- 350 full-time, tenure-line faculty members
- 3,600 undergraduate students

Indiana University-Bloomington uses big, bold numerals to send an entirely different message:

- 550+ Academic Programs and 200+ Undergraduate Majors
- 125+ Research Centers and Institutes
- 2200+ Students Study Overseas Every Year

Baccalaureate Colleges tend to use lots of pictures of individuals and various events that stress a sense of community. Research Universities take the opposite approach. They focus on the breadth of their activities. As such, they tend to use the limited real estate on a homepage to tell a different set of stories:

- "Could Bird Brains Lead to Human Cures? New technology lets BU researcher eavesdrop on avian brains"—Boston University
- "What is Economic Security? Food, shelter and clothing aren't enough, argues a UB-led research study, which says basic needs should reflect possibilities for long-term stability, including a savings plan"—University of Buffalo
- "Stink Bugs. UD researchers look at sweet corn damage caused by stink bugs"—University of Delaware

The bottom line is that the homepage of a college or university is not perceived to be the place to ask and answer any of our key questions: Why do we exist?, What do we want to create?, What do we believe? Perhaps the institutions believe that they have limited time to capture and keep peoples' attention. So, graphics, video clips, outsized numbers are what the institutions believe is needed to build the brand.

So, to what degree is mission, vision, and values or an institution's collective ambition represented on its homepage? Almost zero.

❖ ❖ ❖

There are a few exceptions. Rice University has many of the standard elements on their homepage: "News at Rice," "World Class Research" (with a video about Glioblastoma invading cells), and "Quick Facts" (with big numbers such as "$867,770 endowment assets per student" and "4,300 trees on our campus located in the heart of the nations' fourth largest city"). But right in the middle of all the marketing mania in proud bold letters is "Our Mission:"

As a leading research university with a distinctive commitment to undergraduate education, Rice University aspires to path-breaking research, unsurpassed teaching and contributions to the betterment of our world. It seeks to fulfill this mission by cultivating a diverse community of learning and discovery that produces leaders across the spectrum of human endeavor.

Wofford College provides another illustration. The homepage is populated by a large number of brightly-colored tiles of different size with different fonts. One of the largest is "The Week @ Wofford." Other larger ones are "Pay Us a Visit" and "Academics: Majors and Programs." Smaller tiles include "Terrier Athletics" and . . . "Strategic Vision." The vision link goes to a page that has a beautiful campus landscape and the title "It's Our Wofford" splashed across the page with Wofford's vision statement below. Also on the page is a section "About the Vision" that begins "Imagine a college where each student's experience—academic, residential and co-curricular—is merged together seamlessly."

Finally, at the bottom of the page are two links: one goes to *Strategic Vision: At-A-Glance* and the other to *Strategic Vision document.* The former is a one-page document that aligns the vision to five recommendations that are a set of specific actions. The latter page is a *pdf* of the entire strategic plan that includes, "A History of People and Place," "Vision," "Recommendations," and a "Make it Happen" implementation section. All of this is one click from the homepage.

Again, a homepage may or may not be the place for a full description of the things that should matter most to an institution. But it is also difficult to accept that if there is space to implore the reader to "follow us" on Facebook and Twitter and "see us" on Flickr and YouTube, there might also be room for some acknowledgement and description of an institution's purpose, future, and beliefs.

About ___________

The successful search for information about an institution's mission, vision, and values usually begins with a tab on the homepage. This tab typically states "About" and is followed by the institution's name. While the vast majority of colleges and universities stick with the basics, a few get a little creative with the language:

- "Our DNA" – Boston University
- "Get to Know Tufts" – Tufts University
- "About Mizzou" – University of Missouri

Some of the Items Under the "About" Tab		
Mascot	Campus Tour	Sustainability
Administrative Services	Weather Information	How do I . . . ?
Honor Code	Visitors Guide	Jobs
Facts & Figures	Campus Map	Alumni Hall of Fame
History & Traditions	Transportation	Photo Tour
Accreditation Status	Diversity	Consumer Information
Economic Impact	Visit Us	School Colors

The first issue under the "About" tab is that it is often used as a place to put miscellaneous items. Sometimes the items are in alphabetic order but often they are not. Regardless, the much abbreviated list above gives an indication of the range associated with these items. There are literally dozens of various items that our sample institutions have included here with the feeling that, "If you can't find any other place to stick it, put it under 'About.'" It also suggests that "Mission" or "Vision" or "Values" is often lost in the minutia.

❖ ❖ ❖

A second issue that is apparent involves the definition of terms. There does not seem to be a clear understanding of exactly what mission, vision, and values mean. The terms are often used interchangeably or erroneously conflated. Language is important, especially when it comes to describing fundamental elements of a collective ambition.

An example is Augustana College. Under "About" is "Mission and History." The tendency to talk about the origins of an institution (in Augustana's case 1860) is important. But under the heading of "Mission and History" is a subheading, "Tradition and Vision:"

Augustana College, rooted in the liberal arts and sciences and a Lutheran expression of the Christian faith, is committed to offering a challenging education that develops qualities of mind, spirit and body necessary for a rewarding life of leadership and service in a diverse and changing world.

The words of Augustana's mission statement reflect both tradition and vision. Founded by Swedish Lutheran settlers in Chicago in 1860, Augustana has grown from a small school educating Swedish immigrants into a highly selective college of the liberal arts and sciences. The College honors its roots and its affiliation with the Evangelical Lutheran Church in America. At the same time, Augustana's rich liberal arts environment is enhanced by diversity.

Augustana continues to do what it has always done – challenge and prepare students for lives of leadership and service in our complex, ever-changing world.

Another example is Quinnipiac University. There is a tile on the homepage entitled "History + Vision." The page begins with "Our History" and starts with, "Quinnipiac began as a small college in New Haven in 1929." The second section is labelled "Our Mission" with an opening sentence of, "An education at Quinnipiac embodies the University's commitment to three core values: high-quality academic programs, a student-oriented environment and a strong sense of community."

The problem here, and in other institutions as well, is the casual use of language. The future of a college or university and its collective ambition should be carefully considered and then strategically communicated. Far too often the terms used in conveying that future are applied in a haphazard fashion that belies their importance. The mixing, matching, and conflation of terms creates confusion, disinterest, and ultimately a loss of energy.

Finally, let's say that little or nothing about mission, vision, and values is on an institution's homepage. Perhaps because there isn't enough real estate available or a conscious decision is made about the use of images, stats, and other messaging to help build the brand. The more likely explanation is that the web design process is led by . . . web designers. The questions being asked in the user group meetings, which may or may not include senior leaders, may very well focus on the seemingly more immediate issues of how future students can apply or how current students register for classes. It may follow that such esoteric questions as "What do we believe?" get edged out in the battle by every campus interest group that thinks they need to be featured on the homepage. And it may also follow that lumping together some or all elements of mission, vision, and values under "About" is the next logical choice for many institutions.

But while the active search for mission, vision, and values usually found some success under the "About" tab, there were also many instances in which it did not. The process was then to turn to the Search function in the upper corner of the homepage.

There is certainly plenty of irony surrounding the idea of "searching" for a purpose, a future, and a set of beliefs.

Perhaps the most vexing result of this adventure was when the trail led to a mission or vision statement or strategic plan under a heading of "Administration," "University Leadership," "President" or some other related banner. Unfortunately, this is not an occasional problem. It happens way too often. And it sends a terrible message. Is it the administration's mission? Did the president write the vision? Does an executive team dictate our beliefs?

The University of Utah provides an illustration of narrowly associating mission and vision with the institution's administrative leadership. Under "What" on the homepage is "U Leadership" which contains 13 large photographs with Office of the President at the top of the page. Following the Office of the President breadcrumb you arrive at a page with "News & Events," "Videos," "President's Bio," "Presidential Ambassadors," and . . . the "University's Mission."

Another example is at St. Cloud University where there is "President's Message" under "About Us." In addition to the text of the President's message there is a pullout box titled "Additional Information." On the list that includes "Organizational Chart" and "Institutional Work Plans" is "Mission and Vision."

The University of California, Santa Cruz provides an extreme illustration of this general finding. Its homepage has all the bells and whistles—graphics, videos, and so on. The journey down the rabbit hole begins with "About." Under that tab are such things as "Achievements," "University News," and the "Banana Slug" (mascot). It also has "Administration." That tab is a list of administrative units beginning with "UCSC Chancellor" followed by 14 other units.

Working our way down to "Campus Provost/Executive Vice Chancellor" we find three sections, one of which is UCSC's strategic plan with a bulleted subhead of . . . "Vision." At the same time, under the Chancellor is "Chancellor's Vision for Santa Cruz." It would be nice if the strategic plan's vision—the future we are trying to create—as described by the Provost's office matched the Chancellor's vision statement. Unfortunately, they do not: Two different visions by two different administrators for one institution.

Remember that *Future College* is group, not individual, exercise. From the idea of a "collective" ambition" to a compelling "shared" vision, there is little that can be achieved without massive buy-in.

Connecting the Dots

The next general observation follows from the previous two. Let's say you are able to work your way through the visual noise of a homepage and find an "About" tab. Then you begin your search down what is usually a lengthy (and often miscellaneous) list of items until you find some reference to mission, vision, or values. Or, as just noted, you use the Search function or A-Z Index to find the information.

The earlier discussion of core concepts makes it clear that mission, vision, and values, by themselves, don't accomplish much. It is when they are part of a collective ambition which aligns means and ends that there is a bias for action. It is when the vision creates structural tension with the present that discrepancies lead to resolution through emotional contagion. It is when all these concepts work together, over time, that we achieve a constancy of purpose and momentum. This is a system. Unfortunately, the critical examination conducted here suggests that the notion of "future college" is actually a heap—a series of disconnected elements as opposed to a cohesive whole.

The exceptions are very few and very far between. Appalachian State University and Pacific University are several of those exceptions.

Under "About" Appalachian State University has "Mission, Vision & Values" at the top of the left navigation bar. The link leads to a page that begins with "The Mission:"

Appalachian State University prepares students to lead purposeful lives as engaged global citizens who understand their responsibilities in creating a sustainable future for all.

Importantly, co-located on the same page is the *pdf* of their strategic plan—*The Appalachian Experience: Envisioning a Just and Sustainable Future (2014-2019).* The plan reiterates the mission, the vision, and essential character and core values. It includes a statement of sustainability followed by the plan. There are six Strategic Directions enumerated with each "direction" describing a set of specific action items or initiatives. Finally, each strategic direction is accompanied by a discrete set of Metrics that answer the question, "How will we know if we are successful?" The dots are connected.

Pacific University describes "Origins," "Mission," and "Vision" under a "Who We Are" heading. At the bottom of the page is a link to the institution's strategic plan. The plan reiterates the origins, mission, and vision. It then moves to "Pacific's Core Values:"

• Discovery – Discovery is an integral and essential component of the education process. • Achieving excellence by investing in our people – Excellence is achieved by supporting the people who deliver and receive the university's programs. • Sustainability – The highest quality programs are delivered in a way that is sustainable, both economically and environmentally. • Diversity – Pacific's missions of education, discovery and service require a rich diversity of ideas, people and cultures. • Global community – Graduates are motivated and prepared to contribute to the global community.

Next, the plan enumerates a set of strategic objectives, desired outcomes, and identifies the resources needed to achieve the desired outcomes. It contains a planning timeline and a section entitled "Brutal Facts:"

This vision of the future is not unopposed. Pacific operates in a higher education world that is increasingly connected, competitive and challenging. These environmental factors have been part of trustee and campus presentations and conversations over the last couple of years and include the following • Our traditional applicant demographic is decreasing and thus challenging growth and increasing competition • The recession has had an adverse effect on families and our ability to grow our endowment • Increasing higher education costs and decreasing willingness to pay those costs • Decreasing federal and state aid increase pressure on need for institutional and other aid • The increased federal and state compliance requirements increase operational costs and may challenge growth opportunities.

This "current state" juxtaposed against a vision or "desired state" creates the kind of coherence and connectedness that can move an institution forward. Again, the dots are being connected.

There has been some discussion of using the concept of "institutional effectiveness" to take a more systems approach to what has historically been loose coupling—little interdependency, little coordination, and little information flow. But there is no indication in this analysis that this development has taken hold.

The means to achieving a different and improved future should be contained in a strategic plan. Those plans are not often co-located with mission and vision (wherever they are found). Where are they? The plans—or "How do we get there?"—are sometimes under the "President's" tab. Sometimes they are under an office such as "Planning and Assessment." Usually, the plan needs to be searched for or is found using the A-Z Index.

Finding a strategic plan generally entails a sophisticated game of hide and seek in spite of the fact that the plan should speak both to a vision for the future as well as the strategic choices needed to get there.

Grinnell College provides a useful illustration. Under "About" there is a tab with "Mission and Values." The mission statement is followed by three core values: excellence in education for students in the liberal arts; a diverse community; and social responsibility. But on the left navigation bar is also what appears to be a set of values that also includes teaching and learning and sustainability. Which is it? There isn't anything about vision—What are we trying to create?

Grinnell's strategic plan could be found only by using the Search function. The "Strategic Plan" page begins:

In order to support the College's mission, the strategic plan was developed with six major directions to serve as its guiding framework. Grinnell's model of strategic planning is one of distributed leadership. For each of the six major directions, there are faculty and staff co-leads and a corresponding administrative office.

The problem is that the actual mission isn't on this isolated page. There is no connection between things. There is no coherency. And there is no process being described to show implementation, evaluation, or improvement.

Few institutions, certainly not just Grinnell, seem to be able to connect the dots into a coherent whole that describes how an institution will take responsibility for creating its own future.

Currency

A final observation concerns a disturbing lack of currency—that is, the tendency is to produce a mission or a vision or a plan and then, seemingly, walk away. *Future College* is a dynamic process that imbues the institution with energy and direction. It creates structural tension and invites resolution. But that is not what most institutions appear to be doing. Instead, there is a one-time exercise of drafting a mission and perhaps including a vision and set of values. A plan is produced and appropriately archived. But there is little evidence to suggest that there is a connection to the current state of affairs, daily decision-making, and the need to show constancy of purpose.

An illustration of what should be happening is provided by Linfield College. Under "About Linfield" is a series of items. At the top, however, is "Mission Statement." Linfield College advances a vision of learning, life and community that:

- ***Promotes intellectual challenge and creativity,***
- ***Values both theoretical and practical knowledge,***
- ***Engages thoughtful dialogue in a climate of mutual respect,***
- ***Honors the rich texture of diverse cultures and varied ways of understanding,***
- ***Piques curiosity for a lifetime of inquiry,***
- ***And inspires the courage to live by moral and spiritual principle and to defend freedom of conscience.***

Right below the mission statement is a "Strategic Plan" link that reveals the plan—*Enhancing the Student Experience: Linfield College's 2012-18 Strategic Plan.* The plan itself has three themes and goals as well as implementation principles and timelines. The inclusion of implementation principles and timelines give a strong suggestion that efforts will be made to keep the themes and the associated action items current.

But more importantly, the left navigation bar—under the strategic plan—includes separate annual updates that enumerate *specific* accomplishments linked to *specific* goals. The annual update also includes "Next Steps" which identify, again under each goal, what the college is intending to do in the future.

Another illustration is Montclair State University's strategic plan, *Connecting to Tomorrow: Vision, Creativity, Adaptability* (2011), which "outlines a set of key challenges and actions for ensuring the University's future success." The document outlines five broad goals that form a collective vision:

1. Connecting students with a successful future
2. Connecting people and ideas
3. Connecting to place
4. Connecting globally
5. Meeting challenges and opportunities on the way to tomorrow.

Below the plan (*pdf*) is a series of progress reports. The most recent report, *December 2014 Strategic Plan Progress Report*, describes updates in an animated version such that the reader can flip the pages. So, while the strategic plan is static, the impact of the plan is dynamic.

In both of these instances the institutions are telling its stakeholders that "creating our own future" is a vibrant, on-going process that requires that they take responsibility for continuous improvement.

Most colleges and universities don't bother. When annual progress reports are seen they are usually a set of accomplishments that aren't connected to the vision or the plan. They are marketing pieces. Dashboards are similar. They are often used to establish transparency and to create an appearance of accountability but, again, they are not often connected to a mission, vision, or strategic initiatives.

There is also the situation in which the institution has every intention of creating a dynamic process. Central Connecticut State University (CCSU), for example, has a "University Mission" under "About." It has a strategic plan that is co-located with its mission statement. The planning page begins:

The Strategic Plan is based on the University's statement of mission and vision and four distinctive elements of CCSU's identity. The Plan comprises eight broadly defined goals and an extensive series of objectives aimed at realizing those goals and advancing the University.

Elements of Distinctiveness—CCSU identifies the following as distinctive elements within the Connecticut State University system of four constituent universities:

1. ***International Education***
2. ***Workforce and State Economic Development***
3. ***Community Engagement***
4. ***Interdisciplinary Studies and Cross-Curricular Initiatives***

At the bottom of the page is a critical link: "The president's Report Card on the progress toward the goals of the strategic plan can be downloaded by clicking here." The CCSU Strategic Plan Report Card enumerates planning objectives, the goals, the current metric, and then assigns a letter grade—e.g., B-, A, C+.

The problem is that the one and only report card is dated 2011.

❖ ❖ ❖

3

Mission

Why do we exist?

This seems like an obviously important question—Why do we exist? That is because of its scope and ubiquity. Great philosophers—Aristotle, Kierkegaard, Hume, and Nietzsche—have seen purpose as the preparation for doing what is right and worthwhile. Psychologists such as Maslow and Jung have described how individuals can proceed through life from lower-level needs to their full potential. For Maslow, that ultimately involved other people: "Self-actualizing people are, without one single exception, involved in a cause outside their own skin, in something outside themselves . . . " In very challenging times, the leaders of countries—Abraham Lincoln, Winston Churchill —have relied on a sense of destiny to pull people together and endure tragic events.

Mission or purpose is also of critical importance to organizations. It is the primary source of achievement. Purpose makes people feel their work is worthwhile and builds morale and energy levels. As such, it is bigger than any particular tactic employed or strategy this is developed. The renowned thought leader, Nikos Mourkogiannis, has passionately described this in his book *Purpose: The Starting Point of Great Companies* (2006). He notes that strategy is a step-by-step path toward optimal results. Early on he uses the case study of Enron which had many, many strategies. But strategies are the means; they cannot be an end in themselves. An end is a reason. And Enron, like many failed or flailing enterprises lacked a reason—"it lacked purpose."

Finally, it is imperative to reinforce the idea that mission or purpose is the catalyst. It is the beginning. If it is perceived as a stand-alone concept then it will fail its charge. It needs to be connected. Again, Mourkogiannis:

"An organization with a strong sense of purpose does not just make people feel better. It also creates a strong sense of direction and obligation. Indeed it raises morale at least partly because it creates this sense of direction. This combination of energy and direction makes it effective at stimulating action."

This discussion.is particularly important to institutions of higher education for three reasons: one is historical, the other is environmental, and the third is practical.

The first reason is that colleges and universities have historically been viewed as being mission-centric institutions. Many of the most influential books on higher education over the centuries—Newman's *The Idea of a University* (1873), Kerr's *The Uses of the University* (1963), Bloom's *The Closing of the American Mind* (1987)—have grappled with various aspects of higher education's fundamental purposes. Most recently, such books as *Designing the New American University* (2015) and *Redesigning America's Community Colleges* (2015) have taken an even more forceful approach to rethinking some of the basic tenets associated with higher education in the 21st century.

A second reason that mission statements are so critical to our discussion is that the current environment requires it. It was noted in the Introduction that we are experiencing a high velocity environment which demands that institutions become more reflective about who they are and what they are trying to achieve. Simply, purpose needs to align with exogenous factors such as product positioning, price sensitivity, and labor market analysis so that the institutions remain relevant and sustainable.

Making decisions about fundamental reasons for existence (mission) while ignoring the environmental conditions within which those decisions are made is almost certain to lead to disaster.

The final reason—practicality—deserves a bit more explanation. There are three different types of work in organizations: non-value-added work, value-added work, and business-value-added work. The first, non-value-added work is the kind of scrap, rework, needless complexity, breakdown, and delay that is characteristic of poorly performing organizations. It is simply the inability to efficiently and effectively transform inputs into outputs that end-users want or need. It is a leaky hose associated with the current Completion Agenda.

Next there is "value-added" work. That is the work individuals and institutions do that really is transformative in nature. It is the benefit that is produced. Student and program learning outcomes, if accomplished, represent the best of our institutions adding value to individuals and, ultimately, to society.

The final type is "business-value-added" work. This is the effort that we must put in for the purpose of keeping the doors open. Paying bills, filling out regulatory forms, and responding to legal issues are all things that need to be done in order to keep the organization functioning.

Higher education in this country has a significant "business-value-added" enterprise: It is called accreditation. The quality assurance processes under which services and operations of the institutions are evaluated by external bodies to determine if applicable standards are met remain fundamental to their existence. If you aren't accredited, you really aren't in business because the institution cannot offer its students federal financial aid.

❖ ❖ ❖

A synopsis of mission-related standards and language of the six regional accrediting agencies can be found in Appendix B. Analyses of these documents yield an important constant: *every institution must have a mission statement.*

By themselves, these statements are business-value-added work. They are simply something that you have to have in order to keep the doors open and the lights on. But as was noted in the previous chapter on Core Concepts, ideas such as collective ambition and constancy of purpose are really about "adding value" as the means to help institutions advance. Having a mission statement is surviving and is a necessary but insufficient condition to create positive change in our colleges and universities. Thriving, in contrast, requires that institutions "be on a mission."

Mission Work: Evaluative Criteria

A more detailed analysis of Appendix B is needed to help in the critical examination of the 141 colleges and universities. That analysis resulted in a set of four mission-related elements—domain, process, alignment, and effectiveness—that appears in the standards of the accrediting agencies.

The Domain Described

It is one thing to mandate that an institution should have a purpose; it is another to begin to enumerate what elements should be included in it. Some accreditors are more succinct in their description of what an institution's mission should contain. For example, the Southern Association of Colleges and Schools (SACS) states:

> ***The institution has a clearly defined, comprehensive, and published mission statement that is specific to the institution and appropriate for higher education. The mission addresses teaching and learning and, where applicable, research and public service.***

Others take a more prescriptive approach to how an institution should describe its mission. The Northwest Commission on Colleges and Universities (NWCCU), for instance, devotes considerable effort to this issue of "core themes" within its standard on mission:

The institution articulates its purpose in a mission statement, and identifies core themes that comprise essential elements of that mission. In an examination of its purpose, characteristics, and expectations, the institution defines the parameters for mission fulfillment. Guided by that definition, it identifies an acceptable threshold or extent of mission fulfillment.

Later on, NWCCU enumerates a specific component to its mission standard targeting core themes:

The institution identifies core themes that individually manifest essential elements of its mission and collectively encompass its mission.

Other accreditors focus on such elements as the institution's constituencies, the needs of society, and priorities and vision for the future.

The most extensive description of the domain of an institution's mission is offered by North Central Association's Higher Learning Commission (NCAHLC). It includes the following:

The mission document or documents identify the nature, scope, and intended constituents of the higher education programs and services the institution provides.

- ***The institution understands the relationship between its mission and the diversity of society.***
- ***The institution addresses its role in a multicultural society.***
- ***The institution's processes and activities reflect attention to human diversity as appropriate within its mission and for the constituencies it serves.***

The institution's mission demonstrates commitment to the public good.

- ***Actions and decisions reflect an understanding that in its educational role the institution serves the public, not solely the institution, and thus entails a public obligation.***
- ***The institution's educational responsibilities take primacy over other purposes, such as generating financial returns for investors, contributing to a related or parent organization, or supporting external interests.***
- ***The institution engages with its identified external constituencies and communities of interest and responds to their needs as its mission and capacity allow.***

The Process Used

A second mission-related element that is common to all accreditors is the idea that there needs to be a process involved. For a mission to be useful to an institution it has to have a certain provenance—that is, it can't just appear whole cloth in a catalogue.

The first part of the process suggests that institutions need to follow steps that are comprehensive and inclusive. Several illustrations include:

. . . clearly defined mission and goals that are developed through appropriate collaborative participation by all who facilitate or are otherwise responsible for institutional development and improvement. **Middle States Commission on Higher Education (MSCHE)**

The mission statement is developed through a process suited to the nature and culture of the institution . . . **(NCAHLC)**

A second component is that the mission, once developed through the appropriate process, needs to be formally approved (and supported) by a governing entity. This, of course, is part of our original observation that all accreditors require that institutions have mission statements and that those mission statements are approved. This is part of the business-value component of mission statements. Simply having a mission, and having it approved, does nothing other than keep the institutions open for business.

The final process piece is both value-added and very much emphasized by all accreditors: communication. The mission statement must be developed through an inclusive process, approved by a governing board, and it then needs to be broadly and effectively communicated. Several examples include:

> ***The institution's mission is set forth in a concise statement that is formally adopted by the governing board and appears in appropriate institutional publications.*** **New England Association of Schools and Colleges (NEASC)**
>
> ***The institution has a clearly defined, comprehensive, and published mission statement that is specific to the institution and appropriate for higher education.*** **(SACS)**

The Nature of Alignment

The third aspect of mission statements that is common to all six accreditors is one that aligns the mission with other activities within the institutions. This is, of course, the real essence of value-added activities because it suggests that a well-developed, well-communicated mission statement can have a real beneficial effect in colleges and universities.

The first type of alignment described is the one between a mission statement and specific goals of the institution. For example, MSCHE's mission standard states:

The institution's stated goals are clearly linked to its mission and specify how the institution fulfills its mission.

Another broadly-stated alignment that is often discussed by accreditors is the link between mission and operations. SACS states:

The mission statement is current and comprehensive, accurately guides the institution's operations . . .

The next alignment component involves the linkage of mission with the programs and services that the institution offers. NCAHLC describes the connection in the following way:

The institution's academic programs, student support services, and enrollment profile are consistent with its stated mission.

Another critical alignment that is also described by NCAHLC is one that connects mission to planning and budgeting:

The institution's planning and budgeting priorities align and support the mission.

Finally, one accrediting agency—New England Association of Schools and Colleges—has taken the most comprehensive, value-added, approach to mission by expressly connecting the purpose of the institution, Standard One, to many other Standards:

- *Standard Two (Planning and Evaluation)—The institution undertakes planning and evaluation to accomplish and improve the achievement of its mission and purposes. It identifies its planning and evaluation priorities and pursues them effectively.*
- *Standard Three (Organization and Governance)—The institution has a system of governance that facilitates the accomplishment of its mission and purposes and supports institutional effectiveness and integrity.*
- *Standard Four (The Academic Program)— The institution's academic programs are consistent with and serve to fulfill its mission and purpose. The institution has a system of governance that facilitates the accomplishment of its mission and purposes and supports institutional effectiveness and integrity.to fulfill its mission and purposes.*
- *Standard Five (Faculty)—The institution develops a faculty that is suited to the fulfillment of the institution's mission. Faculty qualifications, numbers, and performance are sufficient to accomplish the institution's mission and purposes.*
- *Standard Six (Students)—Consistent with its mission, the institution defines the characteristics of the students it seeks to serve and provides an environment that fosters the intellectual and personal development of its students.*

The Evaluation of Effectiveness

The final element of mission that accreditors discuss involves an assessment process that seeks to evaluate the effectiveness of the mission. In several instances this evaluative component is embedded in the Mission Standards themselves:

The institution engages in ongoing, integrated, and institution-wide research-based planning and evaluation processes that (1) incorporate a systematic

> ***review of institutional mission, goals, and outcomes; (2) result in continuing improvement in institutional quality; and (3) demonstrate the institution is effectively accomplishing its mission.* (SACS)**
>
> ***. . . periodic Assessment of mission and goals to ensure they are relevant and achievable.* (MSCHE)**

Other times, however, this evaluative component is stated separately, as part of another Standard. For example:

> ***Standard 4: Creating an Organization Committed to Quality Assurance, Institutional Learning, and Improvement—The institution engages in sustained, evidence-based, and participatory self-reflection about how effectively it is accomplishing its purposes and achieving its educational objectives.* Western Association of Schools and Colleges (WASC)**
>
> ***Standard Two: Planning and Evaluation—The institution undertakes planning and evaluation to accomplish and improve the achievement of its mission and purposes.* (NEASC)**

The most robust example of "evaluation of effectiveness" is offered by NWCCU. It book-ends Standard One (Mission, Core Themes, and Expectations) with Standard Five (Mission Fulfillment, Adaptation, and Sustainability). The following introductory language is emphatic about the emphasis being placed on a continuous improvement process:

> ***Based on its definition of mission fulfillment and informed by the results of its analysis of accomplishment of its core theme objectives, the institution***

develops and publishes evidence-based evaluations regarding the extent to which it is fulfilling its mission. The institution regularly monitors its internal and external environments to determine how and to what degree changing circumstances may impact its mission and its ability to fulfill that mission. It demonstrates that it is capable of adapting, when necessary, its mission, core themes, programs, and services to accommodate changing and emerging needs, trends, and influences to ensure enduring institutional relevancy, productivity, viability, and sustainability.

Findings on Mission Statements

The most important reason to analyze mission statements within our sample of colleges and universities is, as noted previously, because they are "must haves"—every other aspect of what might be an institution's collective ambition is optional. But in order to be accredited you simply must have a mission statement that is appropriately communicated to the public. It follows, then, that almost every institution in the sample had a mission statement that was accessible on its website (even though it sometimes took the Search function to find).

The analyses that follow looks at our three institutional categories (Baccalaureate Colleges, Research Universities, and Master's Colleges and Universities) by the four criteria just described (domain, process, alignment, and effectiveness).

Baccalaureate Colleges

One of the more interesting findings across the entire critical examination of college and university mission, vision, and values statements occurs in the subcategory of public liberal arts colleges. The number of institutions in the sample (and in the population) is quite small. That is understandable. There is a bit of a disconnect between the idea of a public institution that might lean toward larger classes and workforce education and the idea of a more intimate education that is not pre-professional in orientation.

If the domain of a mission statement involves setting boundaries and describing exactly what the purpose of the institution is, it might follow that these institutions need to do an extraordinarily good job of "explaining themselves." Perhaps the best illustration of this is offered by University of Wisconsin, Parkside:

The University of Wisconsin-Parkside is committed to high-quality educational programs, creative and scholarly activities, and services responsive to its diverse student population, and its local, national and global communities.

To fulfill this mission, the University of Wisconsin-Parkside will:

- ***Offer high-quality academic programs rooted in the tradition of a liberal education in the arts, sciences and professions, responsive to the occupational, civic and cultural needs of the region, and actively seek the continued input of all stakeholders.***
- ***Generate, disseminate and apply knowledge through research, professional and creative activity that benefits communities throughout the region and the world.***
- ***Attract and retain a diverse and multicultural population of students, faculty, and staff.***
- ***Foster a teaching and learning community that provides opportunities for collaborative faculty, student, and staff interaction in support of excellence.***
- ***Utilize technology creatively and effectively in courses, programs, and services.***
- ***Prepare students to be successful in their professional, civic, and personal lives.***
- ***Provide programs that meet the intellectual and cultural needs of people throughout their lives.***
- ***Provide and share in cultural and intellectual activities in partnership with our local and regional communities.***

In comparing this mission to what accreditors are generally looking for—intended constituents, programs, role in society, and so on—this is a remarkably comprehensive effort. It covers a lot of ground in a relatively concise fashion and for that reason is useful in supporting institutional decision-making.

Several other public institutions also offer robust mission statements that emphasize distinctiveness in even more concise ways:

New College of Florida—*New College offers a liberal arts education of the highest quality in the context of a small, residential public honors college with a distinctive academic program which develops the student's intellectual and personal potential as fully as possible; encourages the discovery of new knowledge and values while providing opportunities to acquire established knowledge and values; and fosters the individual's effective relationship with society.*

Western State Colorado University—*Western State Colorado University fulfills its statutory mission by promoting intellectual maturity and personal growth in its students, and graduates citizens prepared to assume constructive roles in local, national and global communities. Western helps its students develop the skills and commitments needed to continue learning throughout their lives and strives to elucidate the connections unifying academic domains, which have traditionally existed separately: the sciences, liberal arts and professional programs*

Private liberal arts colleges have a rich tradition in this country. That tradition is evident in the examination of their mission statements. Many institutions actually overlay "Mission" with "Tradition" while others begin the description of their purpose with a history lesson:

Grinnell College—*When Grinnell College framed its charter in the Iowa Territory of the United States in 1846, it set forth a mission to educate its students "for the different professions and for the honorable discharge of the duties of life."*

Kenyon College—*Over the 185 years of its life, Kenyon College has developed a distinctive identity and has sought a special purpose among institutions of higher learning. Kenyon is an academic institution.*

Another interesting result is the length of the mission statement. Unlike a vision which should be memorable and focused (and brevity is a benefit), the length of a mission statement is of lesser importance. Still, it is worth noting the range in the sample institutions which ran from Kenyon College's 746-word statement to Kalamazoo and Goucher's much more parsimonious efforts:

Kalamazoo College—*The mission of Kalamazoo College is to prepare its graduates to understand better, live successfully within, and provide enlightened leadership to a richly diverse and increasingly complex world.*

Goucher College— *Goucher College is dedicated to a liberal arts education that prepares students within a broad, humane perspective for a life of inquiry, creativity, and critical and analytical thinking.*

In spite of what accreditors want, there is little evidence of any of the Baccalaureate Colleges, public or private, attending to and describing the process used to develop, approve, and evaluate their mission statements. At the very least it would seem to be important to document the approval mechanism. For example, at the end of Gettysburg College's mission statement it states, "Jointly prepared by the Middle States Self-Study Steering Committee and the Faculty Council, Fall Semester 2002. This statement was adopted by the Gettysburg College Board of Trustees on January, 2003."

Describing the nature of an inclusive process used to develop the mission and enumerating a specific communications plan to ensure that stakeholders are aware of the institution's purpose is also not usually done. As noted in General Findings, while the mission was often found on the website under "About" the other option was to use the Search function. In those instances, the mission was usually linked to a *pdf* of the college's printed catalogue. This hardly seems adequate for what are supposed to be mission-driven institutions.

The most important way in which the nature of alignment is expressed in a mission is not in the mission statement itself but rather how it is used to make decisions and create opportunities for constancy of purpose.

Unfortunately, most institutions do not do this. The tendency is to find an isolated Mission statement under "About XYZ College." In some instances a strategic plan is co-located near the mission statement and then, in even fewer instances, the strategic plan begins with explicit references to mission, vision, and values. For the most part, Baccalaureate Colleges are guilty of producing pretty plans, overflowing with flowery text, and sprinkled with nostalgic shots of the past and current students chatting under trees in a picture-perfect quadrangle. Too often, the strategic plan itself immediately focuses on describing a set of priorities that are not linked to the most fundamental of all organizational questions, "Why do we exist?"

A useful example of strong alignment is offered by Augustana College. In the Preamble to their *Augustana 2020 Strategic Plan* it states, "*Augustana 2020* will strengthen our mission to educate students for a changing world, developing and promoting skills and values more crucial than ever 21st century." The plan itself consists of three student-centered strategies and, again, later in the Preamble it says, "The guiding principle in developing our three strategic directions has been to focus on competitive strategies, asking about major, achievable directions that advance Augustana's mission."

Union College also explicitly states in the beginning of its strategic plan that, "The 2013 Strategic Plan will further Union's mission as a scholarly community, which educates students to be engaged, innovative and ethical contributors to an increasingly diverse, global and technologically complex society."

Juniata College begins its *Courage to Act: The Plan for Juniata College* with a set of "Animating Principles" that includes both the vision and a mission statement: "Juniata's mission is to provide an engaging personalized educational experience empowering our students to develop the skills, knowledge and values that lead to a fulfilling life of services and ethical leadership in the global community."

The evaluation of effectiveness, the final element of what accreditors look for in mission statements, is almost never directly described on institutional websites. One might infer that if an institution, like Gettysburg College, specifically notes when the current mission was approved by its governing board, that some prior evaluative step took place. Another indirect process can also be inferred. If an institution begins its strategic plan with a description of mission, vision, and values and then proceeds to align such a collective ambition with specific priorities, it is operationalizing the kind of alignment that accreditors require. If it goes on the describe the means by which the institution is going to measure success in accomplishing those priorities then there might be an indirect evaluation of mission involved as well.

Both Augustana College and Juniata College, from above, describe this type of assessment. Augustana does it by linking "Evidence of Success" metrics to every "Action Plan" under each of the three strategies in *Augustana 2020.* Juniata College enumerates five strategic priorities in its strategic plan. Each priority is followed by a situational analysis, then key initiatives, and, finally, "Measures Indicating Success."

Unfortunately, this type of reflection is decidedly the exception, not the rule.

❖ ❖ ❖

To summarize, private Baccalaureate Colleges tend to conflate mission and tradition. It is as if the answer to the question "Why do we exist?" is "because we have existed since 1846."

While a sense of history and tradition is certainly important, it may be problematic when helping stakeholders fully understand the institution's role in a high velocity environment in which change is a constant. This issue may also be influencing the other mission-related elements, specifically the idea that mission helps to drive a strategic planning effort and needs to be evaluated as part of a dynamic continuous improvement process. The public liberal arts colleges, it should be noted, present an interesting case study when it comes to describing their domain. Perhaps because of the politics of public funding or simply being such a scarce good, they seem to work extra hard to explain their existence.

Where these institutions excel is in the area of domain. They tend to talk a lot about the kind of students they want to graduate and their role in society. Some of these institutions are quite good at making "purpose" a personal concept and, as described, making the idea of community come alive. Others, such as Carleton College, find ways—again, at a personal level—to make a mission something more than a statement dutifully reprinted in the front of the college catalogue. Under "About Carleton" there are statements on Carleton's mission, vision, values, and goals. But next to the text is a flash video. The header states, "Watch Carleton College students describe in their own words what they believe to be the Mission of the College." Dozens of students manage to make Carleton's mission their own.

Research Universities

The language associated with mission statements in research universities tends to be quite expansive. Johns Hopkins Universities refers to "knowledge for the world," Rice University "produces leaders across the spectrum of human behavior," and Tufts University seeks to graduate students who "distinguish themselves as active citizens of the world."

Perhaps the idea is that if your domain—the nature and scope of the institution—is the world and everything in it, then the language needs to reflect that. Also, it might suggest that the more words you use the less importance they have. Several examples from the public sector include:

University of California, Santa Cruz—*UC Santa Cruz is a leading research university with a tradition of innovation in the education of students—built on values of social and environmental responsibility.*

University of Rochester—*Learn, Discover, Heal, Create—and Make the World Ever Better*

The privates can be equally as thrifty in the number of words used to describe their expansive reach:

Dartmouth College—*Dartmouth College educates the most promising students and prepares them for a lifetime of learning and of responsible leadership through a faculty dedicated to teaching and the creation of knowledge.*

Emory University—*Emory University's mission is to create, preserve, teach, and apply knowledge in the service of humanity.*

In aggregate, though, public research universities appear to devote a great deal of effort to carefully describing their boundaries—what they do and, conversely, what they do not do. Given the nature of their legislative stakeholder's political and financial interests, perhaps it is understandable that they would be more precise in their language. The University of Wisconsin-Madison is an example of this. The institution enumerates a detailed set of eight "musts" that describe such specifics as, "Embody, through its policies and programs, respect for, and commitment to, the ideals of a pluralistic, multiracial, open, and democratic society."

Another illustration of this necessity to be abundantly clear about public institutions' scope can be seen in Stony Brook University's mission statement:

The University has a five-part mission:

- *to provide comprehensive undergraduate, graduate, and professional education of the highest quality;*
- *to carry out research and intellectual endeavors of the highest international standards that advance knowledge and have immediate or long-range practical significance;*
- *to provide leadership for economic growth, technology, and culture for neighboring communities and the wide geographic region;*
- *to provide state-of-the-art innovative health care, while serving as a resource to a regional health care network and to the traditionally underserviced;*
- *to fulfill these objectives while celebrating diversity and positioning the University in the global community.*

While not universal by any means, public research universities are much more likely to describe the process by which their purpose and collective ambition was created. A good example of this is in University of Connecticut's *Creating Our Future: UConn's Path to Excellence.* The introductory section enumerates the mission:

The University of Connecticut is dedicated to excellence demonstrated through national and international recognition. Through freedom of academic inquiry and expression, we create and disseminate knowledge by means of scholarly and creative achievements, graduate and professional education, and outreach.

With our focus on teaching and learning, the University helps every student grow intellectually and become a contributing member of the state, national, and world communities. Through research, teaching, service,

and outreach, we embrace diversity and cultivate leadership, integrity, and engaged citizenship in our students, faculty, staff, and alumni. As our state's flagship public university, and as a land and sea grant institution, we promote the health and well-being of citizens by enhancing the social, economic, cultural, and natural environments of the state and beyond.

Next, the document goes on to describe the institution's core values followed immediately by a section, "The Planning Process," that provides specific insight into how the plan was developed. It begins:

In 2013, UConn launched a comprehensive process to develop a new academic vision to identify specific goals and strategic initiatives, and realize our aspiration to become a top flagship university recognized excellence in breakthrough research, innovative education, and engaged collaborations with state, community, and industry partners.

North Carolina State University's strategic plan, *The Pathway to the Future*, takes a similar approach. The plan begins with "Our Foundation" that includes the "NC State Mission," "NC State Vision," "NC State Values" and then moves to "NC State's Strategic Planning Process." It details the formation of nine task forces. The University of Kansas describes its eight work groups and planning committees and goes on to explain how 104 white paper proposals were used to inform their four strategic initiatives: Sustaining the Planet, Powering the World; Promoting Well-Being, Finding Cures; Building Communities, Expanding Opportunities; and Harnessing Information, Multiplying Knowledge.

The nature of alignment—again, an important aspect of missions that accreditors are looking for—seem to be much more prevalent with public research universities. UC Santa Cruz is one of those institutions (across all institutional types) that seeks to articulate a dynamic process by describing the implementation of a mission-driven plan. Under each of its six goals it enumerates a series of actions to show what happens by stating, "As the projects below are implemented beginning in Spring 2015, pages for each will provide regular updates on project leads, scope, timelines, progress, and metrics."

This is a much more coherent approach to creating your own future. Most of these institutions, at the very least, place their mission, vision, and values statements at the beginning of their strategic plans. A few are even more explicit. For example, the strategic framework for the University of Wisconsin-Madison, *For Wisconsin and the World*, has subtitle of "Focusing a Great University on Its Core Mission, Public Purpose, and Global Reach." *One Mizzou: 2020 Vision for Excellence*, the University of Missouri's strategic plan, places its mission statement on the inside cover in a bold font that extends across the page.

Finally, there is the evaluation of effectiveness. Colorado State University's plan begins with vision, mission, and values followed by each strategic planning area, objective, goal, strategy, and then "related metrics." University of Delaware also connects the same pieces in its *Delaware Will Shine*. Each strategic initiative is followed by a set of priority recommendations and "measuring our progress." The University of Kansas's plan, *Bold Aspirations*, begins with its mission as a public international research university: "to lift students and society by educating leaders, building healthy communities, and making discoveries that will change the world." It goes on to describe goals, strategies, and actions. The final, and comprehensive, section of *Bold Aspirations* is called "Measuring Progress" and tracks the success of the four strategic initiatives. University of South Florida has a separate section of its plan entitled "Gauging Our University's Progress" that begins, "As the University of South Florida continues to raise its stature as a pre-eminent research university measured through carefully and critically tracking . . . " and is then displayed in a "Performance Dashboard."

While there are illustrations of Research Universities that enumerate mission, vision, and values and strategic priorities, and then describe a series of metrics that are used to measure the success of those initiatives, there are few that make the link directly back to the mission.

One exception is Oregon State University's Strategic Plan 3.0—*Focus on Excellence.* It begins with "Our Mission" and "Our Vision." The mission statement is:

As a land grant institution committed to teaching, research, and outreach and engagement, Oregon State University promotes economic, social, cultural and environmental progress for the people of Oregon, the nation and the world. This mission is achieved by producing graduates competitive in the global economy, supporting a continuous search for new knowledge and solutions and maintaining a rigorous focus on academic excellence, particularly in the three signature areas: Advancing the Science of Sustainable Earth Ecosystems; Improving Human Health and Wellness; and Promoting Economic Growth and Social Progress.

Towards the end of the document, a chart entitled "Metrics Associated with Institutional Mission and Goals" enumerates a set of 16 metrics such as "Six Year Graduation Rate," "Licensing Revenues," and "Total R&D Expenditures" along with baseline rates, annual performance measures, and targets. This is an overt effort to take responsibility for continuous improvement. It is asking the questioning "How will we know if we are successful in fulfilling our mission?," and then putting in place a discrete set of metrics to answer that question.

❖ ❖ ❖

In the beginning of this chapter it was noted how important it was for a mission or purpose to not just make people feel good but to "stimulate action." This is where research universities, particularly the publics, appear to shine. Perhaps it is because of their need to be accountable to system boards or legislators. Perhaps it is because they have the size to devote additional resources to connecting the dots between means and ends. Regardless of the cause, accreditors and stakeholders are likely to be pleased to see such comprehensive, integrated efforts.

Master's Colleges and Universities

As has been noted, these are workhorse institutions. While community colleges certainly enroll more students, for those seeking a baccalaureate degree many student attend these institutions. As the California State University homepage proclaims:

The CSU is a leader in high-quality, accessible, student-focused higher education. With 23 campuses, 460,000 students, and 47,000 faculty and staff, we are the largest, the most diverse, and one of the most affordable university systems in the country.

While there are positives associated with this distinction, it presents some challenges when it comes to identifying the nature and scope of services. Baccalaureate Colleges focus on history, tradition, and a sense of community. They articulate (institutional) student learning outcomes well—here are the knowledge, skills, and abilities you will have when you connect to society. Research Universities speak to the span of their impact in research and economic terms. They use "global" language.

Master's Colleges and Universities struggle to explain themselves because, to a degree, they are caught in the middle. Some, especially the publics, tend to lean toward the research university prescription (without the language of research and terminal degrees) by focusing on short mission statements that emphasize their comprehensiveness:

Bloomsburg University of Pennsylvania—*Bloomsburg University of Pennsylvania is an inclusive comprehensive public university that prepares students for personal and professional success in an increasingly complex global environment.*

The University of Northern Iowa—*The University of Northern Iowa provides transformative learning experiences that inspire students to embrace challenge, engage in critical inquiry and creative thought, and contribute to society.*

Others tend to pull from the Baccalaureate College playbook by focusing more narrowly on students and community:

Northwest Missouri State University—*Northwest Missouri State University focuses on student success—every student, every day.*

James Madison University—*We are a community committed to preparing students to be educated and enlightened citizens who lead productive and meaningful lives.*

Some public institutions do a kind of "mashup" and attempt to place both of these perspectives—one expansive and the other intimate—in one mission statement. Appalachian State University and Winthrop University illustrate this approach. Appalachian's mission statement begins: "Appalachian State University prepares students to lead purposeful lives as engaged global citizens who understand their responsibilities in creating a sustainable future for all." But that expansive worldview is followed by:

Our location in the distinctive Appalachian mountain town of Boone, North Carolina, profoundly shapes who we are. As a constituent institution of the University of North Carolina, we fulfill our core academic missions of teaching, scholarship, and service in ways that honor our geography and heritage.

Winthrop produces even more mission whiplash in one "200-year spanning" sentence:

Building on its 19th century origins as a distinctive women's college, the Winthrop University of the 21st century is achieving national stature as a competitive and distinctive, co-educational, public, residential comprehensive, values-oriented institution.

But the greatest tendency here is to add and add some more. Marshall University provides an illustration. It begins its 518-word mission statement with "Marshall University is a multi-campus public university providing innovative undergraduate and graduate education that contributes to the development of society and the individual." The institution goes on to enumerate a series of bulleted sections:

Marshall University will . . . **(11 bullets)**
Marshall University faculty will . . . **(6 bullets)**
Marshall University staff will . . . **(3 bullets)**
Marshall University students will have the opportunity to . . . **(5 bullets)**
Marshall University administration will . . . **(6 bullets)**

The private Master's Colleges and Universities have perhaps the greatest challenge when it comes to describing their domain. Like the publics in this Carnegie classification, there is the general problem of being neither an intimate liberal arts experience nor the international brand name of a research university. They also face the additional challenge of not having the same value proposition—that is, "bang for the buck"—that a state university has. They need to be crystal clear about their purpose—who they serve and why.

Drake University's mission statement provides a useful example of how to be explicit and distinctive when asking and answering the "Why do we exist?" question:

Drake's mission is to provide an exceptional learning environment that prepares students for meaningful personal lives, professional accomplishments, and responsible global citizenship. The Drake experience is distinguished by collaborative learning among students, faculty, and staff and by the integration of the liberal arts and sciences with professional preparation.

While Drake speaks directly to the issue of integrating liberal arts and careers, Rochester Institute of Technology (RIT) begins its mission with a specific effort to describe a very different approach:

RIT's mission is to provide a broad range of career-oriented educational programs with the goal of producing innovative, creative graduates who are well-prepared for their chosen careers in a global society.

In general, these institutions cannot afford to be wispy or open-ended when describing their intentions. They need to make choices and then describe the nature of the choices they have made to various stakeholders.

The process criterion required by accreditors also generated some straightforward observations. At the very least, the process portion of mission statements should denote who contributed to the development of a mission-driven strategic plan and when it was approved by a governing board. A good example is Stetson University. In addition to the standard elements, they describe the process used—the groups involved—and then state, "In May 2014, this inclusive process culminated in the approval of the 2014-2019 Strategic Map by the Stetson University Board of Trustees, with implementation beginning in fall 2014." A video of some of the proceedings is even provided. Similarly, Webster University describes their planning process as having "engaged hundreds of members of the university community in thousands of hours of work" and then proceeds to document them—two trustee retreats, four theme teams, seven work groups, and so on. Again, a snappy video is used to provide highlights.

Alignment, again, is a critical element of what accreditors look for in their mission standards. Many of these institutions fulfill that requirement by enumerating their mission, vision, and values at the beginning of their strategic plans. Some are explicit about that relationship. California State University East Bay, for example, has a "Mission and Strategic Planning" section on their website which directly links "purpose" with a bias for action to fulfill that purpose. After describing their purpose, they unequivocally state:

The University's strategic planning process is intended to support this mission - to lead to greater organizational effectiveness, better use of resources, and achievement of University goals and objectives. Through the use of evidence to inform decisions and assessment to evaluate the results of actions, Cal State East Bay is able to guide its future with confidence.

One of the most comprehensive efforts to align mission with other activities is offered by Drake University. The institution's strategic plan begins with the mission, vision, and values mentioned earlier. But before jumping into a standard explication of goals and strategies, the institution adds the following powerful introductory statement:

Our vision for Drake University's future is grounded in a pervasive sense of institutional mission, as articulated in the University's Mission Statement and discussed in detail in Drake's Mission Explication. As a binary pair, we must be certain that there is a clear and direct line between our mission and our vision for Drake's future—they are inextricably linked. The Mission and Vision together provide the energy and direction for the University's development—in essence, we are driven by the Mission and drawn forward by the Vision. Our ultimate metric in measuring the success of both our

> ***vision for Drake University in 2017 and our strategic plan to realize that vision is the quality of the student experience—the learning outcomes of the "exceptional learning environment" promised in the Mission Statement.***

The Appendix—Strategic Plan Implementation—pulls everything together by describing "Goal Working Groups," "Strategic Plan Implementation Groups (SPIGS)," and "Engage-ment & Communications Strategies." Again, this is the difference between simply having a mission statement as mandated by accrediting agencies and using the mission to catalyze movement.

In these two areas—process and alignment—there were different tendencies with privates and publics. The private institutions tend to see their purpose and planning as an opportunity to differentiate themselves from the rest of the herd. There is much more flash involved. The publics take a more functional approach with a greater focus on meeting various requirements and expectations. It is the necessary work associated with living in an era of accountability.

Finally, these institutions don't appear to be any better at evaluating the effectiveness of their mission statements than the other two categories. Those institutions that describe specific measures of success tend to be in the public realm. Framingham State University, as an illustration, concludes their strategic plan with an appendix—Indicators of Success—that identifies a series of metrics with a baseline (2012) and strategic targets (2017). Similarly, St, Cloud State University's plan has six strategic themes with each having a series of strategic objectives followed by a set of key performance measures.

The real challenge here is threefold: (1) often time the metrics are not explicitly linked to the plan's strategies; (2) the metrics are not kept current such that a trend is apparent; and (3) the metrics themselves are buried deep within the bowels of the institution's website. The result is that the answer to the question "How will we know if we are successful?" usually is . . . "We really don't know."

Mission Summary

There is no more fundamental question for an organization than, *Why do we exist?* It follows that accreditors—the official arbiters of quality—are forceful in requiring institutions to describe their missions. They are equally adamant that the mission is communicated to stakeholders. And they also want to know what the mission entails, how it was developed, how it aligns with planning activities, and how the mission is evaluated.

In a very practical sense, it was also noted that having a mission with a discrete domain can help save institutions from . . . *themselves.*

It is in our DNA to want to expand boundaries, to test limits, and to reimagine who we are. But in today's new normal of "doing more with less" that adventurism can be disastrous. Mission creep is a very real thing.

In our current higher education environment, though, it is more a matter of "mission seep." Expanding a mission beyond its initial goals is one thing but in a resource-constrained environment those added endeavors are often paid for out of existing budgets. The flow of resources to these initiatives—the seeping—constrains existing programs and services with institution-wide mediocrity being the inevitable end state.

This problem is evident in many of today's news stories and public conversations about higher education as well as debates on campuses themselves. For example:

- The search for resources has led many public state institutions to recruit both out-of-state and international students. While the additional tuition dollars help to balance the budget, state officials and other stakeholders have questioned the strategy as a betrayal of a state-supported mission.

- In the hunt for prestige and the perceived need to be competitive, colleges and universities have allocated more and more of their scarce resources to amenities—climbing walls, lazy rivers, and fashionable dining experiences—with the result of making the front page of newspapers and magazines in a time of $1 trillion of student debt.
- As enrollment in humanities decline, many liberal arts colleges have been faced with the decision to embed internships into their programs, bolster career centers, or consider adding some professional programs.
- For all colleges and universities, the amount of time, energy, and resources to commit to online education is another question: some of the smaller institutions simply see it as irreconcilable with their mission statements.

One high-profile example is athletics. A *Chronicle of Higher Education* (October 24, 2010) article by Charles Clotfelter entitled, "Is Sports in Your Mission Statement?" directly addressed the issue:

"Whether the benefits of big-time college sports programs are worth the costs may still be a subject worthy of robust debate. But faculty members and administrators do a disservice to themselves and their institutions by pretending that the sports-entertainment complex is no more significant to a university's functioning than are its dining halls or art museums. Such lack of candor is out of step with the imperative we teach in classrooms and practice in laboratories—to seek and speak the truth."

This is not an esoteric debate. In December of 2014, the president of the University of Alabama at Birmingham announced that he was eliminating the university's football program. He noted that the university had doubled its annual support for athletics over the previous decade, from $10 million a year to about $20 million, while outside funding remained the same at about $3 million. It was clear to him: He refused to take even more of the university's money away from its academic and health-care missions to support the football program. In

June, 20015, after months of uproar and objections from students, alumni, and other supporters, the president reversed his decision and said he would reinstate the team.

The uproar in Wisconsin is an even more headline-grabbing example. When Governor Scott Walker introduced his state's budget in the beginning of 2015 he redefined the University of Wisconsin's system mission statement, making "training the workforce" ascendant and eliminating the "search for truth" as the institution's guiding principle. He was accused of seeking to eliminate the "Wisconsin Idea," the notion that at the core of a great state university should be, above all else, a search for truth and the application of knowledge for the benefit of students, state, and society.

After using the proposal to gain other concessions (and in the face of serious pushback from angered Badger supporters) he meekly retracted the proposed changes to the mission statement.

All these of these issues, large and small, are mission related. They speak to the fundamental purpose of the institutions. While it is easy to get caught up in the immediate matters of enrollment and budgets, it is worth noting that such challenges are often symptoms. The fundamental issues are usually deeper and involve developing and communicating a very precise understanding of an institution's fundamental purpose. And by default, if a college or university cannot get its arms around being purpose-centered, it will necessarily become comfort-centered.

Questions to Ask

This *Fieldbook* needs to provoke dialogue to be effective as a pragmatic guide for decision-making. Such dialogue is often best stimulated through a series of questions. One way to organize the questions is by dividing them into three parts: past, present and future. The first—"Looking Back"—is an attempt to begin by reflecting. It is, simply, important to understand how we got here. Next is a series of question about "The Current Situation." A situation analysis is another attempt to put the brakes on the prevailing fire-fighting paradigm. Slow down, breath deep, and understand what is at stake.

Finally, most of the questions are "Looking Forward." That reflects the importance of the role that purpose plays in developing and executing a collective ambition.

Looking Back

- How was the current mission statement developed?
- What were the pros and cons of using that approach?

The Current Situation

- What are the most important elements of this institution's mission as it currently exists?
- How is the mission being used to inform daily decisions about service, programs, and resource allocation?
- If you were to ask stakeholders the question "Why do exist?," what type of feedback would you receive?
- Where and how is the mission communicated?

Looking Forward

- What does your accrediting agency say, specifically, about mission statements?
- Who should be involved in the dialogue about your institution's purpose?
- How and when should that conversation take place?
- What are the barriers to having an honest and transparent conversation about your mission?
- How can the mission be used to inform daily decision-making and resource allocation?
- What is the best way to communicate the mission and make it real to people?
- How will you be able to evaluate the mission and its effectiveness?

❖ ❖ ❖

4

Vision

What do we want to create?

Mission and vision often get lumped together in higher education. We saw that in the General Findings chapter. Institutions will have a "Mission" header under "About" and then, almost as an afterthought, include "Vision" underneath the general description of purpose. Sometimes, the opposite occurs. There will be a lofty statement about where the institution is headed and then, later, a more workman-like accounting of the programs it offers. But mission and vision represent to very different concepts.

The most straightforward difference is one of tense. If a mission answers the question, "Why do we exist?," it follows that it is a matter of current importance. That currency suggests that it has real value in making daily decisions about the programs and services that are offered by an institution. As noted, without a strong sense of common purpose there is a tendency for individuals and interest groups to make decisions that place self-interest over the collective good. Mission creep (and seep) can be a very real result because in higher education, by nature, we want to say "yes" and we want to "add."

It is also true that mission statements tend to reflect the past and why "traditions" are so often co-located with a mission statement on webpages. Understanding the circumstances under which an institution was formed and its seminal purpose is important. It produces a sense of history and longevity. It gives everyone a sense that they are a part of something permanent. And in a high velocity environment with shifting trends and quick-hitting fads, a sense of permanence is certainly not a bad thing for any organization.

But there is a downside, too.

As we noted in the earlier chapter, a mission statement is prescribed by accrediting agencies. If you want access to federal financial aid, you need to be accredited, and if you are accredited *you will* have a mission statement that meets the standards of the accreditor. Those standards include various aspects of a domain description, process, alignment, and effectiveness. The result can be, and often is, a fairly comprehensive exposition that can be referred to at times and be invoked when necessary. It can be used to inform difficult choices. And the mission can change—although with glacier-like speed—over time as part of an evaluative process.

So far, so good.

But it is clear that the bias of a mission statement is towards the past tense. As such, what it doesn't provide is any sense of future aspirations or, "What do we want to create?"

A vision statement exists in the present but it attempts to describe a different tomorrow. It doesn't have to defer to the past. It doesn't need to respond to a mandate. What it must do is inspire.

The core concept of structural tension is at work here. An "actual state" can easily be reflected in our initial question, "Why do we exist?" But without a forward-leaning, future-engaging question, preserving the status quo becomes the default dynamic. The result is no real discrepancy between yesterday, today, and tomorrow. And we know that without that discrepancy there is no structural tension; and without that tension there is no effort to create resolution—or a bias for action.

❖ ❖ ❖

A second important issue follows from this. If a vision is critical to helping build momentum in an institution, then it needs to be "compelling" and "shared." This is the conclusion of Peter Senge in his seminal work, *The Fifth Discipline*, introduced earlier. Senge describes a set of disciplines that define a learning organization, one of which is building a shared vision. He notes:

"A shared vision is not an idea. It is not even an important idea such as freedom. It is, rather, a force in people's hearts, a force of impressive power. It may be inspired by an idea, but once it goes further—if it is compelling enough to acquire the support of more than one person—then it is no longer an abstraction. It is palpable. People begin to see it as if it exists. Few, if any, forces in human affairs are as powerful as shared vision."

This is decidedly not something that is dutifully printed in a course catalogue. It isn't meant to be trotted out every six or ten years for an accreditor's approval. It must not be only an agenda item for the board to approve as part of a long-range strategic planning effort. The kind of vision that helps to propel a college or university into the future is one that people carry around in their hearts and minds. It is a living, breathing idea about what is possible. The problem, of course, is that being able to describe that future—in a way that is both compelling and shared— is extremely challenging.

Make it Stick: Evaluative Criteria

So, how do we create the future? One very helpful approach has been provided by Chip and Dan Heath in their popular book, *Made to Stick: Why Some Ideas Survive and Others Die* (2007). The authors analyzed hundreds of ideas that stuck—like Velcro—and then identified six principles that tend to improve "stickiness." They are: simplicity, unexpectedness, concreteness, credibility, emotional, and stories. These principles, when applied to higher education, can provide the evaluative framework needed to ensure that ideas can be transformed into compelling, shared visions.

Simplicity

There is power in simplicity. A vision that rambles on and on will not capture the imagination of anyone. It is really true that, ultimately, more is less. Yes, it is also true that some stakeholders may be pleased about explicit references to them in a long, drawn-out vision statement. But while individual constituents might be happy in that situation, the organization as a whole loses out. To strip an idea down to its core, as the Heaths' suggest, we must be "masters of exclusion." The exercise is to prioritize relentlessly such that the essence is pure and palpable. As such, it is not a matter of just being short or catchy. A vision isn't a logo. The analogy is more like a distillation process in which many elements are "boiled off" until the very essence reveals itself.

Unexpectedness

Most of what we do every day in life is a matter of repetition. We drive the same way to work, we order the same thing in restaurants, and we express the same opinions over and over again to anyone who will listen. We have expectations about all these things and more. As such, days and weeks turn into a blur of undifferentiated thoughts and activities. But if we want to remember something—such as a vision—we need to violate people's expectations. By stating the obvious and repeating words like "quality" and "excellence" we ensure that the reader will lose focus and interest. As noted by the authors, for an idea to endure, we need to generate interest and curiosity. That doesn't happen when we string together a lengthy set of expected words and pedestrian phrases and then call it a vision. Instead, we need to disrupt our tendency to anticipate what will be written or said based upon our own experience and the context.

Concreteness

Made to Stick's authors are particularly critical of organizations here: "Mission statements, synergies, strategies, and visions—they are often ambiguous to the point of being meaningless." Ambiguity is the enemy of stickiness. The tendency is to give into flowery language and industry buzzwords. We feel the need to explain and elaborate in ways that ultimately obscure the essence of the idea. But nuance, tone, and shade aren't memorable. What people remember—and what makes certain ideas stick—are ideas that have some bulk, mass, or . . . concreteness. Perhaps the best way to understand this stickiness principle is: If you can visualize it you can remember it. For example, it is difficult to remember the idea of "liberty," it is easy to remember the statue, Lady Liberty, which occupies the entrance to New York's harbor.

Credibility

The question here is, how do you make people believe your ideas? Some part of the answer to that question is wrapped up in the statement . . . consider the source. The source of an idea has a lot to do with whether the idea is perceived as credible. But it goes beyond that. Ideas that stick are ones that seem believable. They seem real. A vision statement that is credible is realistic about expectations while, at the same time, aspirational in how it describes the future. The language is believable and creates a sense of legitimacy and truth. Without that credibility, the future being described is quickly dismissed as being unattainable or misdirected. And once an idea or vision is dismissed, it is also forgotten.

Emotional

Believing is one thing, but caring about something is also critical to its stickiness. How do we get people to care about our ideas? For the authors of *Made to Stick*, the answer is pretty simple: We make them feel something. The more abstract the concept—the more generic and detached it is—the more likely it is to go in one ear and out the other. Similarly, a vision statement that doesn't elicit an emotional reaction is one that isn't likely to be compelling. A mission statement, as has been described, can be almost purely functional in nature and be sufficient as part of a collective ambition. The vision, though, is about a "desired" state. As such, it needs to go beyond the functional such that the discrepancy is real and creates the necessary structural tension. For a vision to be effective, you need to feel it and then be able to pass that feeling on—emotional contagion.

Stories

The final quality that improves stickiness involves turning a passive idea into one that enhances active dialogue. Passivity is really about a lack of engagement. Ideas that connect in a way that encourage sharing necessarily mean that people—both sender and receiver—will remember them. And when we talk about a compelling "shared" vision, it doesn't just mean that we agree on the vision. It is more than that. Sharing, when it comes to a vision, means that people understand the essence of the future that is being described and find opportunities to relate that future to their everyday professional lives. It becomes part of who they are and they express it on a regular basis in productive conversations. Finally, this is a self-fulfilling prophecy. The more we are engaged in pursuing the vision, the more we tend to share it; and the more we share it, the more we believe in our destination or desired state.

To summarize, the six qualities of ideas—*and visions*—that stick are:

- Simplicity—How do we strip a vision to its core?
- Unexpectedness—How do we capture people's attention with the vision?
- Concreteness—How do we help people understand the vision?
- Credibility—How do we get people to believe in the vision?
- Emotional—How do we get people to care about the vision?
- Stories—How do we get people to act on the vision?

There is an important bottom-line to this analysis. The most effective vision statements really do rely on many of these elements of stickiness. They get to the point. They capture one's imagination by being unpredictable. They are real. They make people believe and elicit passion. And then people want to talk about and share their experiences.

When you put all that together what "sticky" visions do best is to create a sense of specialness. In effect, the answer to the vision question never involves the cautious response that typically involves what an institution has in common with others in their institutional types. Rather, it is a description of their own vibrant and distinctive future that is both compelling and shared by all its stakeholders.

Findings on Vision Statements

Before applying the evaluative criteria to our colleges and universities, it is worthwhile to make a series of broad observations. The first is simply the presence or absence of a vision statement. As has been made clear, a mission statement is mandatory for accreditation purposes and can usually be found somewhere on higher education websites (even if you have to use the Search function to track down a page that is embedded in the college catalogue). Visions are a lot less prevalent:

Institutional Types	# of Institutions	# with Visions	% with Visions
Baccalaureate Colleges- Public	9	5	56
Baccalaureate Colleges-Private	33	15	46
Research Universities- Public	24	16	67
Research Universities- Private	15	5	34
Master's Colleges/Univ.-Public	36	26	73
Master's Colleges/Univ.-Private	24	13	55
Total	141	80	57

This is obviously a problem. It is impossible for an institution to demonstrate their responsibility to stakeholders if they can't describe the future they are trying to create. While six in ten institutions in the sample had vision statements that could be found, 40 percent could not. The potential fallout is more acute for public institutions—which do seem to fare slightly better in both Research Universities and Master's Colleges and Universities categories. If these institutions shy away from describing what future they want to create, there are plenty of political entities and state agencies that are eager to do it for them.

The second observation involves the issue of tense and how it is used in the visions that were found.

A significant failing is the need for some institutions to describe their destination as a place at which they have already arrived.

This is ego talking—"We are great. We have been in the past and expect to be in the future, too." The vision is written as a done deal. Here are illustrations from three institutions:

We are known and respected for preparing our graduates to be exceptionally successful in navigating an increasingly complex and uncertain world . . .

A destination university internationally recognized as an inquiry-driven, ethically engaged, and diverse community . .

Through active discovery, applied knowledge, and creative interaction, we positively transform our students and the communities . . .

The obvious problem here is the lack of structural tension. It is not possible to have any discrepancy if the ideal state and actual state is the same thing. And without discrepancy there is no tension; and without structural tension there is no need to invest in a resolution—or a bias for action. It paraphrases Pogo's famous line: "We have met the enemy and he is us." Instead, this is "We have met the future and it is our present."

Fortunately, this thinking doesn't dominate our institutions. A word frequency analysis across all institutional types found that "will" was almost as prevalent as "student" in vision statements. Many institutions found interesting alternatives to the use of "will" as a description of the future they were seeking to create:

Carleton College—***The College's aspiration is to prepare students to lead lives of learning that are broadly rewarding, professionally satisfying and of service to humanity.***

College of Wooster—***Our collective endeavor is to prosper as a distinguished independent liberal arts college, to thrive as a vigorous intellectual community, and to create a reputation that reflects our achievements . . .***

Colorado Mesa University—***It is the year 2020 and Colorado Mesa University has continued to mature into . . .***

Framingham State University—***Our vision is to create a vibrant and innovative educational environment that is dedicated to academic excellence . . .***

Bentley University—***By its centennial celebration in 2017: Bentley University is known nationally and internationally as a business-focused center of learning . . .***

Baccalaureate Colleges

These institutional types obviously spend a good deal of time using the words "liberal" and "arts." They also tend to use "community" a lot. Interestingly, the word is usually used not in the context of a community they serve but, rather, a description of the institution itself.

Simplicity is seen in the vision statements of two institutions. The first is Juniata, a small, private institution in the middle of Pennsylvania and, the second, Fort Lewis College, a public institution in western Colorado:

Juniata College—***Juniata College will be known for inspiring citizens of consequences who understand the world in which they act.***

Fort Lewis College—*We strive to be the finest public liberal arts college in the western United States.*

Of course, shorter does not necessarily mean better, more distinctive. But the contrast between these forward-leaning, single-sentence visions stands in stark contrast to Bennington College's 271-word "History and Vision" that begins, "In the early 1920s . . ."

An illustration of how credibility can aid stickiness is provided by Bucknell University. Their vision statement begins with the sentence, "To provide students with the premier undergraduate experience in American higher education." While this is certainly succinct, it also smacks of over-the-top grandiosity. What moderates such a beginning is a short means-end description which follows as the resolution portion of our structural tension model:

Bucknell will offer an academic program that is challenging and distinctive, with the capacity to prepare its graduates for successful personal, professional, and civic lives in the 21st century. Bucknell's residential life and co-curricular activities will fully support its academic program. This integrated environment for student learning and growth, enhanced by diversity in all its forms, will build connections to a global society. In doing so, Bucknell will emerge from a place of strength to a position of pre-eminence within American higher education.

Evoking an emotional response helps an idea, and a vision, to stick and be distinctive. One institution uses the concept of community described above to provide a passionate tug.

Moravian College—Thus, we envision a strong and vital Moravian which, in the future will be:

- *A community of the great embrace, welcoming men and women from all walks of life, locally, nationally, and globally;*
- *A community of liberal learning where scholar, intellectual curiosity and creative expression invigorate all facets of our lives;*
- *A community of service, which equips and empowers men and women to serve others with professional skill, grace, and integrity, including those who live out their lives on the periphery of society;*
- *A community of wise stewards, who care for and enhance our treasures of heritage, people and place for generations to come;*

As such, Moravian will be a leader within higher education—a community of choice for students, faculty and administrators, a model of excellence.

The University of Puget Sound provides an interesting example of vision that is both a story and encourages story-telling. The vision begins:

The key for us at Puget Sound at this moment in our history is not to invent a new story about ourselves, but to understand where our story has taken us and how it might further unfold. Ours cannot just be an account of institutional transformation; it must also be a story of distinction. This is our challenge: to tell that story and make it true by defining our character and the difference it makes. This is the thread that will lead us into the next chapter of a great story and will empower us to define the future and Puget Sound's place in it.

The vision goes on to speak about its distinctive combination of a strong liberal arts curriculum and innovative interdisciplinary programs and adds a compelling phrase, "A Puget Sound education is not something you get, it's something you do and someone you become."

While there are examples of Baccalaureate Colleges with strong, "sticky" vision statements, this examination suggests there is a significant problem, too. As described in the Introduction, higher education exists in a high velocity environment. Part of the political and economic drumbeat concerns what some people believe is the need for practical, job-ready degrees. To them, we can't afford the luxury of the liberal arts and their wispy, vague skills such as critical thinking, enlightened citizenship, and cultural competency. Others might argue that such a skill set is more important now than ever. Few people stay in the same job. Reinvention is the key. Or as Rosabeth Moss Kantor of Harvard Business School has famously stated: "Make yourself employable, not just employed."

And yet a disproportionate number of liberal arts colleges didn't even have a vision statement that could be found. Those that were found tended to be rooted in the history and tradition of the institution. The word frequency analysis found that words like "respected," "premier," "recognized," "reputation," and "excellence" were dominant. Few visions were unexpected. None were concrete. There were no Statues of Liberty.

In 1990 there were many more liberal arts colleges than there are today—actually, there were more than 600 then and less than 300 in the current Carnegie Classification of Arts and Science Baccalaureate Colleges. So, the most compelling question for these institutions really is, "What do you want to create?"

Research Universities

As one would hopefully expect, the word "research" dominates the vision statements of Research Universities. The context follows as well. While liberal arts colleges speak about their "communities," research universities tend to use other language that reflects a different view—"global," "international," and "world." Words such as "innovation" and "innovative" were used throughout the visions. The idea that the institutions sought to be "preeminent" was also widespread.

Quite a few research universities had rather concise statements that reflected an appreciation for brevity:

Rensselaer Polytechnic Institute—*Rensselaer pursues this goal: To achieve greater prominence in the 21st century as a top-tier world-class technological research university with global reach and global impact.*

Carnegie Mellon University—*Carnegie Mellon will meet the changing needs of society by building on its traditions of innovation, problem solving, and interdisciplinary.*

North Caroline State University—*NC State University will emerge as a preeminent technological research university recognized around the globe for its innovative education and research addressing the grand challenges of society.*

At the other end of the range were institutions like University of California, Santa Cruz and University of Connecticut. With a strategic plan that is entitled "Envision UC Santa Cruz," the institution begins with a present tense, mixed message:

The University of California (UC), Santa Cruz, is a pre-eminent public research university. Our campus is distinguished by our high-impact research and our commitment to diversity, social justice, the environment, and educational opportunity. Our innovative approach to research and experiential education provides a transformative student experience.

The vision statement then goes on to state that the institution is "recognized broadly for our areas of distinction and research impact" in 375 words.

The University of Connecticut asks the question "What makes a great university?" in the introduction to their vision statement. It isn't an easy question. Indeed, UConn goes into some length (701 words) in attempting to describe many aspects of greatness.

The principle of unexpectedness, as just noted, seems to be a challenge for institutions of higher education. We seem to want to focus on what we have in common with other institutions, not what differentiates us from others. One example, however, is offered by Georgia Tech University.

Georgia Tech will define the technological research university of the 21st century. As a result, we will be leaders in influencing major technological, social, and policy decisions that address critical global challenges. "What does Georgia Tech think?" will be a common question in research, business, the media, and government.

Vision statements are usually stated in terms that reflect how the institutions view their own futures. It is a rarity for an institution to aspire to a vision of how they wish to be perceived by others. It is unexpected.

Concreteness remains a challenge for this institutional type. There are lots and lots and lots of reference to "excellence" in the vision statements of research universities. But what does that mean? One way to demonstrate concreteness is to embed a specific goal into the vision. The University of Arkansas has done that—a dream and a deadline:

By 2021, the University of Arkansas will be recognized as one of the nation's top 50 public research universities with nationally ranked departments and programs throughout the institution.

As we have shown, ideas and visions that stick are also credible. People need to believe that the future is not just lofty language or a Hallmark card of good intentions. One way to do that was illustrated earlier: enumerate a strong connection between means and ends. The University of Rochester describes itself as "A University of the Highest Order." That is pretty lofty. The vision goes on to state, "Founded as 'an institution of the highest order' and guided by the motto 'Meliora' or 'Ever Better,' the University of Rochester will help solve the greatest challenges of the 21st century by . . ." That is an end—a big, bold destination.

What then follows is a series of "means" statements that include the following:

- ***Creating innovative connections among education, humanities, music, the social sciences, science, engineering, and health science.***
- ***Strengthening support for a dynamic faculty dedicated to teaching, mentoring, research, clinical care, and the creative and performing arts.***
- ***Embracing our leadership position in Rochester and the nation by making our community a model for partnership among academic, civic, cultural, health care, and business organizations***

For an illustration of how to get people to care about an idea which is at the very heart of emotional contagion, it is useful to return to Georgia Tech University which was discussed earlier in this section. At the end of their strategic plan—*Designing the Future: A Strategic Vision and Plan*—they add a section entitled "The Path Forward." In it, the following language is used:

Imagine an Institution that:

- ***Attracts world-class students. Faculty, and staff with diverse backgrounds;***
- ***Is preeminent in research and teaching, and known for innovation;***

- ***Is a place where top global decision makers go to find thought leaders and experts to solve multi-faceted problems in science, technology, engineering, and business;***
- ***Has the agility, vision, and mind power not only to face the future, but also to design it;***
- ***Strives for excellence in all that it does; and***
- ***Is known the world over as simply the best in its chosen areas of distinction.***

That is the Georgia Tech of the future, the Georgia Tech we strive to create.

What is important in this "imagine" statement is the lift, the emotional contagion that is created. There is no comfort or complacency here. They haven't already arrived at their destination. The road ahead will be challenging but it is a journey that engages and excites.

❖ ❖ ❖

While these universities provide useful illustrations of how visions can "stick," this institutional type has a fundamental problem.

If, in the world of commerce, liberal arts colleges were the equivalent of smaller, family-run businesses, then Research Universities would be the equivalent of holding companies—the Berkshire Hathaway's of higher education.

Berkshire Hathaway wholly owns businesses in such disparate sectors as insurance, transportation, real estate, chemicals, jewelry, and clothing. In the same manner, the modern research university is a "multiversity" with many different affiliated research centers, institutes, colleges, and divisions. All of these parts can, and usually do, have distinct cultures as well as different operating policies and practices. The challenge of creating a compelling "shared" vision in such institutions (or holding companies) is significant.

And the fall back is too often something that resembles the vision statement from one of the institutions in our research university sample:

To be an innovative university of creative scholars across a broad range of schools who have a profound impact on one another and the world.

This cannot and will not motivate anyone. It is just a bunch of strung-together words.

Master's Colleges and Universities

As one would expect, the language used in these vision statements is also unique. Words like "engaged," "citizens," "comprehensive," and "regional" are often used to describe the futures these institutions want to create. Interestingly, the private institutions tend to talk more about "national," "global," and "society," which may reflect their need to recruit from a larger pool of potential students. Public master's colleges and universities, in contrast, had the most number of found visions (three in four), which may reflect the perceived need to be accountable to taxpayers.

Like other institutions types, Master's Colleges and Universities have a significant number of institutions that have simple, straightforward vision statements. For example:

Emporia State University—*Changing lives for the common good.*

James Madison University—*To be a national model for the engaged university; engaged with ideas and the world.*

Morehead State University—*We ASPIRE to be the best public regional university in the South.*

Very few institutions here had visions that contained anything that was unexpected. Indeed, if unexpectedness really is a significant part of stickiness, these colleges and universities are Teflon. It is hard work to find anything—words, phrases, structure—that is not predictable. At best, Robert Morris University adds a glimmer of unexpectedness in their vision statement by placing the words "best value" in italics with the specific intention of trying to compete on quality as a function of relative worth:

Robert Morris University strives to become a recognized "best value" leader by providing a highly proactive student engagement learning environment that is focused on producing graduates of consequence and influence in their personal and professional lives.

A trend in higher education—the drive to describe institutional student learning outcomes—may ultimately help institutions become more concrete in describing their aspirations. What accumulated knowledge, skills, and attitudes should students develop during their course of study? Austin Peay State University (APSU) has taken this tact:

APSU's vision is to create a collaborative, integrative learning community, instilling in students habits of critical inquiry as they gain knowledge, skills, and values for life and work in a global society.

Emerson University provides an example of a vision that is unequivocal. Because of that, there is some increased credibility. You tend to believe an institution has put a lot of thought into their view of the future when they are direct and focused:

Our vision for the future is simple and strong: Emerson College aspires to be the world's leading institution of higher education in the arts and communication, infused with liberal arts.

Again, how do we get people to care about an idea or a vision for the future? Most of these Master's Colleges and Universities fail to evoke any sort of emotional response. One institution that attempts to create some passion in their vision statement was Marshall University. All of Marshall's rather lengthy vision ties back to a single idea—"Aiming for Perfection." The vision statement begins:

Aiming for perfection is a state of mind. It is the attitude that we choose to bring to our life's journey. It is the vision that lights our journey as we endeavor to actualize the tremendous potential that lies within ourselves and Marshall University.

It goes on to describe what "Aiming for Perfection" means, first to the institution and second to the individual. The statement says the following about what "aiming" means at the individual level:

On an individual level, aiming for perfection is about developing our minds, our bodies and our spirits to their fullest potential. It is about balance and harmony and pursuing a higher consciousness and purpose. It is about achieving a state of enlightenment that is transcendent. It is about endeavoring to discover the wonder and comprehend the complexity that is life. It is about finding meaning, inspiration and coherence in the ambiguity, uncertainty and chaos of daily life. It is about helping others find their voice and their connection to the world around us.

Finally, there is the principle of story-telling. The more a vision statement has aspects that lend themselves to sharing, the more likely it is that the future being described will be personal and real to individuals. The University of Findlay has their "UF Distinction" that begins by stating, "The University of Findlay will become a leading Midwestern university characterized by the following three watch phrases." These "watch phrases" describe the institution's Heartland Community, Diverse Perspectives, and Transformative Experiences.

Each of these watch phrases can form the basis for stories—e.g., "How exactly do we reflect a Heartland Community?"

The greatest challenge with Master's Colleges and Universities vision statements is the clear lack of distinctiveness. This institutional type, especially the publics, is more likely to have vision statements that could be found on the website. But having a vision statement is one thing while having a vision that is unique, sticks, and creates emotional contagion is something quite different. Being "all things to all people" is not a compelling future.

Below are four institutions (three private and one public) and their four vision statements *in no particular order*:

Institution's Name	Vision Statement
Sacramento State University	____________ *will be an innovative leader the in the delivery of academic excellence and enduring educational value, preparing all students for success in their studies and throughout life.*
Wilkes University	____________*will lead higher education in preparing students for innovative, creative, and successful careers in a global society.*
Alfred University	____________*will provide exceptional educational experiences that transform students and develop innovations through scholarly activities that lead to national recognition and shape the world around us.*

Institution's Name	Vision Statement
Rochester Institute of Technology	___________*will be a recognized leader in education, innovation, and engagement.*

The obvious challenge is to match the vision to the institution. When that exercise becomes a trial-and-error guessing game, it doesn't give you much confidence about an institution's abilities to describe a compelling, shared, and sticky future. And when that desired state is not well-articulated, there is little chance that individuals will share the kind of emotional contagion needed to propel it forward.

Vision Summary

In the world of finance, stock prices generally increase or decrease as a result of changes in *expected* future earnings. In the world of higher education, reputation generally increases or decreases as a result of changes that have *already occurred.* The first "world" tends to look to the horizons for inspiration while the second "world"—our world—often looks in the rearview mirror for affirmation. That is why mission statements and the traditions of the institution are often co-located or even integrated on website. It is why the purpose of the college or university can usually be found somewhere on the site while finding a description of a future or desired state takes a bit of sleuthing.

We are more comfortable talking about what we have accomplished—i.e., how many federal research dollars we have been awarded, how many National Merit scholars we have attracted, or what our enrollment is—than in challenging the status quo as a place that is good . . . but not nearly good enough.

The problem, of course, is that in a high velocity environment an institution this is not adapting and looking to the future is actually losing ground. As such, it is critical that institutions of higher education work hard to develop and describe a vision for tomorrow. But as this critical examination shows, that is much more difficult to say than it is to do. The task of visioning doesn't come naturally to us. It is a struggle. But it must be done.

A useful example of why is provided in a study done Yoram and Edith Neumann and reported in *Inside Higher Ed* (August 5, 2015). The majority of studies of colleges, their CEOs, and leadership skills are single static studies. The Neumann's study, however, included two different snapshots spread over five years with the same sample of 158 presidents and colleges.

Three leadership skills were studied: visioning, focusing, and implementing:

1. Visioning referred to the ability of the CEO to help foresee the future of the college, identify the opportunities that would transform the fate of the college, and conceptualize the long term path for growth.
2. Focusing includes the involvement of constituents in adopting a new vision for the institution through a consultative process.
3. Implementing is directing the operations needed to carry out the plans for the new and the process for realizing its goals.

Each CEO was classified as high versus low for each of these strategic leadership skills. The highest level of strategic leadership profile is a leader who rated high on all three skills (visioning, focusing, implementing). That profile is defined as the Integrator. The lowest rating on the skills is the Maintainer with various types of leaders—with both highs and lows—between these opposing profiles.

The results of the study suggest there is a continual decline in institutional performance when moving from the Integrator through other strategic profiles to the Maintainer:

"College president/CEOs who are Integrators experienced the maximal resource growth, the maximal enrollment growth, and a major improvement in their perceived quality. Integrators had the strongest odds in being associated with positive bottom line outcomes

over time while Maintainers had the strongest odds in being associated with negative bottom line outcomes."

These research results reinforce the theme that has developed throughout this chapter. A college or university performs best when the individuals within the institution share a common vision for the future—one that is compelling, shared, and really, really sticky. Moreover, that desired state provides the tension to propel the institutional forward and overcome the powerful forces of inertia. Maintaining is losing and that usually results in even more efforts to impose various accountability initiatives. In contrast, when we take responsibility for our own future, we move from surviving and reacting to thriving and creating.

Questions to Ask

Like with mission statement in the previous chapter, a group that is deliberating an institution's vision needs additional information in the form of the past, present, and future or where we have been, where we are, and where we should be headed:

These are the questions your group needs to be asking in order to further describe its collective ambition:

Looking Back

- What was the process used to create your current vision?
- Why do you think it was done that way?

The Current Situation

- If you were to ask a broad range of stakeholders about the institution's vision, what language would they use?
- How does the current vision align with the mission statement?
- How is the current vision communicated and used in decision-making?

Looking Forward

- Who should be involved in the process of developing a compelling shared vision?
- How and when should that dialogue take place?
- What about your institution is special and can be used to differentiate it from others in the future?
- Thinking about your institution in four or five years, what should be its defining characteristics?
- What are the barriers to describing your future?
- What is the best way to communicate the vision?
- How will you know if you are successful in developing a compelling shared vision that is helping to move the institution forward?

❖ ❖ ❖

5

Values

What do we believe?

Creating your college's future is, first and foremost, a team sport. Yes, if you do nothing substantive in terms of direction-setting there is a good chance that the doors will still be open in the future and the lights will be on. But that is surviving. It is muddling through. And being in a passive mindset means that the institution will be forced to play catchup—always reacting, always fixing.

We want to be thriving.

We want lots of people believing in somethings larger than themselves. In the broadest sense this means creating a culture that is a set of shared expectations. Culture, then, is really the starting point: It is an organization's self-image. And that self-image is manifested in how the organization conducts its business, treats its employees, customers, and the wider community; the extent to which freedom is allowed in decision-making and considering new ideas; how information and influence is shared through its structure; and how committed employees are towards a common objective. In other words, culture is in the air. It is the milieu within which all the work of the organization occurs.

But culture can also be dissected into rites, rituals, taboos, heroes, symbols . . . and values. Indeed, most organizational scholars who study this area conclude that values—a set of deeply ingrained principles—serve as the cultural cornerstone. Perhaps this notion is best stated by what is considered the classic book on the subject, *Corporate Culture* (1982), by Terrence Deal and Allan Kennedy:

"Values are the bedrock of any corporate culture. As the essence of a company's philosophy for achieving success, values provide a sense of common direction for all employees and guideline for day-today behavior. These formulas for success determine (and occasionally arise from) the types of corporate heroes, and the myths, rituals, and ceremonies of the culture. In fact, we think that often companies succeed because their employees can identify, embrace, and act on the values of the organization."

The very last sentence—*the idea that an organization's success is often a function of employees' ability to identify, embrace, and act on a set of values*—is extremely powerful, indeed.

Several years after Deal and Kennedy's book caused a stir in the corporate world, George Kuh and Elizabeth Whitt produced a thoughtful higher education analog—*The Invisible Tapestry: Culture in American Colleges and Universities* (1988). Their extensive literature review of a broad range of research and writing on culture (in sociology, management, higher education, and so on) arrived at essentially the same conclusion:

"Some institutional values are conscious and explicitly articulated; they serve a normative or moral function by guiding members' response to situations. Most institutional values, however, are unconsciously expressed as themes (e.g., academic freedom, tradition of collegial governance) or are symbolic interpretations of reality that give meaning to social actions and establish standards for social behavior. They often take the form of context-bound values that are related directly to a college's vitality."

Unfortunately, the intervening decades have resulted in scant attention devoted to culture and values. We are increasingly focused on the immediate. There are budgets and enrollment concerns. There are national, state, and regional issues. Studies and reports are coming at us from well-intentioned foundations and less-well-intentioned government bodies. Themes appear to wash over us—doing more with less, demands for accountability, student learning outcomes, and the Completion Agenda.

But one of the best ways to flourish (to be vital) in a hyperactive environment is to be solid and secure about a collective ambition as described in the Core Concepts chapter. The key part of that discussion was that an organization's future wasn't a function of a series of independent elements. Rather, elements such as purpose, vision, core values, and others such as strategic and operational priorities interact in powerful ways.

One of the ways in which mission, vision, and values are connected in higher education is along a head/heart continuum:

Mission ***Vision*** ***Values***

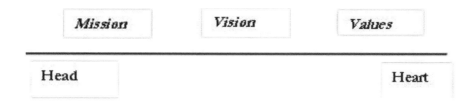

Head **Heart**

As we noted in the Mission chapter, the development and execution of a mission statement is very much an analytical exercise. There are state education codes to consider and accreditation criteria to review. The process needs to be deliberative—*from the head.*

A vision has a strong emotional component. While it needs is to be grounded in the dispassionate exposition of the fundamental purpose of the organization, it also needs to arouse a feeling in individuals. The passion comes from connecting individuals to institutions that create lift and emotional contagion.

Values move us further along the continuum. Since values are essentially about how we want to treat each other, they need to emerge from interpersonal dialogue. Accreditors can't dictate that. The state governing board wouldn't be able to enumerate a set of beliefs. The fact is that individuals don't turn to the college catalogue for clues about how to behave. They look to each other—*from the heart.*

❖ ❖ ❖

This chapter is about getting back to basics. It doesn't get any more basic than asking the question, "What do we believe?" And it is appropriate that it occupies the final leg of our three-legged stool of mission, vision, and values. A mission statement delineates a clear and specific description of an organization's fundamental purpose. A vision presents what the organization wants to become and gives direction to a desired future. But values seek to clarify how individuals within the organization will conduct themselves in order to make the mission and vision come alive. Values are at the heart of any institution's collective ambition.

Belief Systems: Evaluative Criteria

A popular *Harvard Business Review* (2002) article, "Make Your Values Mean Something," by Patrick Lencioni begins with a stark observation:

"Take a look at this list of corporate values: Communication, Respect, Integrity, Excellence. They sound pretty good, don't they? Strong, concise, meaningful. Maybe they even resemble your own company's values, the ones you spent so much time writing, debating, and revising. If so, you should be nervous. These are the corporate values of Enron, as stated in the company's 2000 annual report. And as events have shown, they're not meaningful, they're meaningless."

The evaluative criteria used to assess the mission statements in this critical examination were distilled from the standards of accrediting agencies. That decision was based upon a simple truth: all regional accreditors want their colleges and universities to describe their purpose, show how their communicate it, explain how they derived it, and so on. The importance of "mission" is codified in their standards.

The evaluative criteria used in the previous chapter on vision suggest something quite different. While a mission is by fiat, a vision is by choice. In addition, a vision plays a different role in our collective ambition. It isn't something to be referred to, it is something to be inspired by. The evaluative criteria, therefore, need to reflect that and explains the use of "stickiness" as the tool to assess the vision statements found in the sample institutions.

Values are different, too. As we just saw in the head/heart continuum, the primary way that values are different is that they are almost entirely in the emotional realm. To be effective, therefore, values need to evoke an emotional response with organizations as a whole and with individuals in particular. Values really need to be meaningful.

With this in mind, the criteria used to evaluate the "meaningfulness" of values statement are three: discreteness, differentiation, and authenticity.

Discreteness

A values "statement" is usually a set of values. These values are traits or qualities that are considered worthwhile. They represent an institution's (and the individual's) highest priorities and deeply-held beliefs. In order for such values to be meaningful, though, they first need to be defined in discrete ways. The best way to do that is to recognize that a value has specific components:

- The name of the value
- A clarifying statement that defines terms
- A number of key behavioral attributes

It is difficult for any set of values to be effective in helping to build a strong organizational culture if the values themselves are not well understood and actionable. They cannot mean something if they aren't delineated in clear, concise ways.

Differentiation

Lencioni is explicit about this: "Even executives who take values seriously can sabotage them by adopting blandly nice ideals that fail to differentiate their company from competitors." The same is true in colleges and universities. Values, like visions, involve feelings and one of those feelings speaks to specialness. Those visions that inspire and those values that engage occur when there is a sense of uniqueness about the institution (where it is going) and the individuals (what they believe).

It follows that values such as "quality" and "excellence" are so ubiquitous that they fade into the background. They don't offend but they also don't resonate and engage. They are largely devoid of meaning.

Authenticity

The development of a set of values has little to do with consensus building. They are not "feel good" ideas that result from organizational surveys or customer/user focus groups. They are the result of an iterative process that begins with mission and vision. The questions really need to be hard-edged and targeted. For example, if mission asks "Why do we exist? Then the follow-on values question is "What values do we need in order to fulfill our purpose?" Likewise, if the vision question is "What do we want to create?" then the values question is "What values do we need to achieve our aspirations?"

This suggests the importance of a very real and determined effort to identify and articulate those values. Beliefs that are meaningful are the result of a process of introspection that challenges us to consider and then reveal what matters most. They must feel—and must be—authentic.

Findings on Values Statements

Before enumerating specific findings by institutional types, it is worth discussing several general findings. In the previous chapter it was noted that only about six in 10 institutions had both a mission and a vision identifiable on their websites. That analysis was extended to whether all three elements—mission, vision, and values—could be found for each institution in our sample. The table below shows that approximately one-third of the 141 colleges and universities hit the trifecta: a mission, a vision, *and* a set of values:

Institutional Types	# of Insti-tutions	# with Visions	% with Visions	# with Visions & Values	% with Visions & Values
Baccalaureate Colleges-Public	9	5	56	3	33
Baccalaureate Colleges-Private	33	15	46	10	31
Research Universities-Public	24	16	67	5	21
Research Universities-Private	15	5	34	4	27
Master's Colleges/ Univ.-Public	36	26	73	15	42
Master's Colleges/ Univ.-Private	24	13	55	10	42
Total	141	80	57	47	34

This is an important initial finding because Lencioni concludes his article by stating, "Weave core values into everything." If values statements are declarations that explicitly define how people will treat each other in the institution and how they will interact with their students and communities, they need to be broadly shared. They need to be a fundamental part of an entire range of activities and actions. Indeed, another organizational expert, Kristin Arnold, in her July 1, 2012, blog enumerates a set of behaviors on which values should have impact.

"When values are internalized by the people in the organization, they have meaning and impact on behavior:

- **Values guide every decision that is made.**
- **These organizational values help each person establish priorities in their daily work life. Priorities and actions are grounded in organizational values.**
- **Adoption of the values and behaviors are integrated into the regular performance feedback cycle.**
- **Rewards and recognition within the organization are structured to recognize those people whose work embodies the values.**
- **The organization hires and promotes individuals whose outlook and actions are congruent with the organization's values."**

It is difficult to imagine that a college or university is serious about weaving core values into everything—including decision-making, performance feedback, and hiring—when it appears to be such a challenge to establish if those values are even present.

Again, it isn't that institutions which don't have easily identified values on their website don't have them or haven't created a strong, coherent culture. It is reasonable, however, to think that if you were going to write them down and use them when making decisions, your stakeholders' electronic "home base" would be a great place to start.

Words Used in Values Statements		
1. Integrity	5. Truth	9. Supportive
2. Excellence	6. Ethical	10. Sustainable
3. Respect	7. Quality	11. Dignity
4. Diverse/Diversity	8. Respect	12. Collaborative

A second general finding involves a word frequency analysis of those values statements that were found. Interestingly, there was not a significant difference between institutional types. The names of values that you would expect to be frequently mentioned were, indeed, stated repeatedly. This is disconcerting because it doesn't say a lot about differentiation. The top 12 words (values) are ranked above.

Moreover, the use of words such as "excellence" and "quality" speak to a lack of authenticity. These are lazy terms. When a set of meaningful beliefs don't emerge, the fallback is to use "excellence" in the hopes that saying it will make it happen. In most situations, "excellence" is just a term in a list and fails our discreteness criterion—that is, there is no clarifying statement that defines the term and no serious attempt to identify key behavior attributes.

It appears that some institutions believe that by stating they value "excellence" or that they believe in "quality" that it will somehow just occur. Saying is not doing. And with no behaviors associated with the terms—behaviors that can be measured—the use of such values is simple hyperbole.

Baccalaureate Colleges

It was noted in the Vision chapter that the word "community" was used a great deal, mostly within the context of the institution itself—that is, they tended to see themselves as a community more than an organization. This sentiment is also reflected in how they refer to their values. For example, Allegheny College refers to them as a "Statement of Community" and Goucher College calls them their "Community Principles."

While most liberal arts colleges use some variation on values—e.g., Our Values, Core Values, ABC College Values—there are also other titles being used. For the most part, a mission is called a "mission" and a vision is called a "vision" in our sample of colleges and universities. But values are different. Perhaps it is because they are more personal, from the heart, rather than being more analytically derived—from the head—like a mission statement. For example, Knox College uses "What We Stand For" while Union College begins with "Union College Believes In." In other words, Baccalaureate Colleges tend to personalize their values in ways that reflects their organizational cultures.

Some Baccalaureate Colleges provide case studies on how to bring meaning to values by being discrete with their language. Fort Lewis College, a public liberal arts college in Colorado, is particularly good at linking behavioral attributes to its values. For example:

- ***Student success is at the center of all the College endeavors*** **(note: name of value)** ***. . . Learner needs, rather than institutional preferences, determine priorities for academic planning, policies, and programs. Quality and advising is demanded, recognized, and rewarded*** **(behavioral attribute).**
- ***Connected knowing, independent learning, and collaborative learning are basic to being well educated*** **(note: name of value).** ***The College structures interdisciplinary learning experiences throughout the curriculum to have students develop the ability to think in terms of whole systems and to understand the interrelatedness of knowledge across disciplines*** **(behavioral attribute).**
- ***Evaluation of all functions is necessary for improvement and continual renewal*** **(note: name of value).** ***The College is committed to studying and documenting its effectiveness through assessment*** **(behavioral attribute).**

College of Wooster articulates all three components: the name of the value, a clarifying statement that defines terms, and a number of key behavioral attributes. Specifically, they name a set of values: Education in the Liberal Arts Tradition, A Focus on Research and Collaboration,

A Community of Learners, and so on. But on their website they include a link that says, "Read more about each of these core values." One is disaggregated as follows:

> ***Independence of Thought*** **(note: name of value)—*We are a community of independent minds, working together. We place the highest value on collegiality, collaboration, openness to persons and ideas in all of their variety, and the free exchange of different points of view*** **(note: clarifying statement). *We vigorously champion academic freedom, and seek to sustain a campus culture where the understanding of each is made more complete through an on-going process of dialogue with others who think differently*** **(note: behavioral attribute).**

Of course, Baccalaureate Colleges should differentiate themselves from other institutional types based upon their beliefs. Knox College speaks a lot about the uniqueness of their community in their mission statement. When they turn to answering the "What do we believe?" question they seek to reinforce their distinctiveness (and meaningfulness). First, as we have noted, they don't talk about "Values" but, instead, speak to "What We Stand For." Next, they describe what they stand for in a way that is undoubtedly unique to their institution. Here are two of their beliefs:

- ***Education embraces difference. We seek out opposing views. We pursue the unfamiliar, the overlooked, the alternative. We're polyphonic; we're capable of speaking and thinking and acting in dozens of ways. This is how the world works; this is how innovation happens; this is how you belong to (and create) the future.***
- ***Education works especially well if everyone is, at heart, nice. We try to be nice in the broadest, deepest sense of the word: we smile at people when we pass them; we see the good in others; we make good food and share it. This is what it means to be from a small city in the heart of the country.***

The language being used is exceptional. That is intentional. Knox College, and others, want to and need to establish a community that set themselves apart from other higher education institutions in a highly competitive environment.

Finally, there is authenticity. In addition to being a strong illustration of discreteness, Wooster College does a great job in this area as well. Their "Core Values" begins: "These are the values that govern our shared pursuits, the ideas that we hold true." The language is genuine and is integrated into the College's collective ambition. For example, here is Wooster's vision:

Our collective endeavor is to prosper as a distinguished independent liberal arts college, to thrive as a vigorous intellectual community, and to create a reputation that reflects our achievements. We seek to be leaders in liberal learning, building on our tradition of graduating independent thinkers who are well prepared to seek solutions to significant problems, to create and communicate new knowledge and insight, and to make significant contributions to our complex and interdependent world.

Wooster is being very clear. It cannot seek to create its own future without a cohesive culture that includes the enumerated values that they "hold true."

Goucher College refers to its values in terms of community or "Who We Are." It begins with "Our Commitments to One Another." The phrase is purposeful and effective and is described in the following way:

While working, studying and traveling on behalf of Goucher, we recognize that we represent the Goucher community, and we will conduct ourselves in a manner that reflects the following commitments:

Taking one of those commitments as an example, in this case Respect, it shows that Goucher follows through on their beliefs in very specific ways:

Respect **(note: name of value):** ***We will treat everyone within our community with respect and learn from our differences*** **(note: clarifying statement).** ***When conflicts arise, we will work together to come up with mutually beneficial resolutions*** **(note: behavioral attribute).** ***We also commit to respect and protect the environment on our campus and in the world.***

❖ ❖ ❖

This is an area of a Baccalaureate College's collective ambition where they should excel. They should be able to describe their community in terms and attributes that allow them to differentiate themselves from other institutions of higher education. The authenticity of their beliefs should shine through like a beacon to all current and future stakeholders. By doing so, their values serve as the basis for emotional contagion, a type of virtuous cycle in which actions that reflect their beliefs serve to reinforce their commitments to one another. This provides the kind of positivity and lift in an organization that can help it thrive in a dynamic environment.

Research Universities

As with Baccalaureate Colleges, some Research Universities use a derivative of Values as a header—e.g., "Our Core Values" and "Statement of Values." Unlike the liberal arts institutions, the term "community" is never used. The more prevalent language involves "principles." For example, Emory University has "Ethical Principles" and University of Delaware uses "Guiding Principles."

But this difference in language seems to reflect a deeper challenge. Indeed, where Baccalaureate Colleges have a tendency to be reflective and personal here, Research Universities seem to be challenged by the need to understand and communicate a set of shared beliefs or values for institutions with numerous centers, institutes, and thousands of employees.

The default scenario is easily seen in the first evaluative criterion—discreteness. Indiana University, as an illustration, introduces its Values with the following statement: "Indiana University is committed to the highest standards of ethical conduct and integrity. In pursuing all aspects of the university's mission, the members of the Indiana University community are dedicated to advancing these core values . . ." The first five values (of ten) are listed below:

- ***Excellence and innovation***
- ***Discovery and the search for truth***
- ***Diversity of community and ideas***
- ***Respect for the dignity of others***
- ***Academic and personal integrity***

These values are not clarified or are there any behavioral attributes offered. What does "Excellence and innovation" mean? How is "Discovery and the search for truth" manifested at Indiana? How will the institution know "Respect for the dignity of others" is actually influencing behaviors?

The University of Texas-Austin has taken the first steps in describing (or clarifying) its values but, again, there is not a lot that is actionable:

***Learning* (note: name of value)—*A caring community, all of us students, helping one another grow* (note: clarifying statement).**
***Discovery* (note: name of value)—*Expanding knowledge and human understanding* (note: clarifying statement).**

***Freedom* (note: name of value)— *To seek the truth and express it* (note: clarifying statement).**
***Leadership* (note: name of value)— *The will to excel with integrity and the spirit that nothing is impossible* (note: clarifying statement).**
***Individual Opportunity* (note: name of value)—*Many options, diverse people and ideas, one university* (note: clarifying statement).**
***Responsibility* (note: name of value)—*To serve as a catalyst for positive change in Texas and beyond* (note: clarifying statement).**

But, for the most part, Research Universities struggle to connect the dots here: a name, a clarifying statement, and a set of behavioral attributes.

Are Research Universities able to create meaning through differentiation? Not very well. One prominent Research University states the following under a banner of "Values"—"The university is committed to excellence. It fosters a multicultural environment in which the dignity and rights of the individual are respected. Intellectual diversity, integrity, and disciplined inquiry in the search for knowledge are of paramount importance." The problem of course is that this could be the beliefs of any one of the other 107 institutions in the Carnegie classification of Research Universities (Very High Research Activity).

Another research university in the sample (that actually had a set of values) enumerated them in the following way:

We are absolutely committed to freedom of inquiry—the freedom to think, to question, to criticize, and to dissent. We will pursue the value of excellence in our research and educational missions with the single-mindedness that only great commitments deserve. We will provide our students with the foundations for ethical citizenship and service to others, a respect for differences among people, and a commitment to high standards

of thought and communication. We also will prepare them for rewarding lifelong careers and will imbue in them a continued and permanent desire for the study of knowledge and the search for truth.

It isn't that the values embedded in this statement are particularly good or bad. It certainly isn't that the institution isn't sincere about what it values. The problem is that when the values are so generic and interchangeable with other institutions of the same type, it is difficult to see how they can guide decision-making, establish priorities, influence hiring choices, and so on.

It was noted in the previous chapter that research universities often struggle to describe what they are trying to create. A vision—one that is compelling, shared, and sticks—can be problematic for institutions that have expansive missions and loosely-coupled systems. At times, it seems that every center or college or division is running its own show with little, if any, understanding or concern for an overarching institutional vision that is distinctive and catalyzes movement.

Perhaps a better approach is a heavier reliance on answering the question, "What do we believe?" Brown University invokes a quasi-vision-like statement entitled, *The Brown Difference*:

Our strategy builds on the essential characteristics that distinguish Brown from other leading universities. Brown is both a major research university and an educational institution based upon collegiate values. We believe that education and research reinforce each other and that the best academic programs bring innovative teaching and rigorous research together. Brown is widely known for its open undergraduate curriculum and the close working relationships between faculty and students. Innovative education that recognizes the value of student-centered learning at all

levels – undergraduate, graduate, and medical – is fundamental to our vision of Brown's future.

While this statement violates some of the principles of stickiness, it also obviously suggests that Brown is a different type of Research University. That difference is, perhaps, more clearly articulated in a companion statement, *The Brown Approach:*

We are a community that celebrates intellectual curiosity, creativity, and individuality; appreciates the power of collaboration among individuals with different perspectives, backgrounds, and areas of expertise; and fosters research and education that strive to have a positive influence on society. In an era characterized by sharp ideological divisions, we will continue to cultivate an environment of open debate and informed civil discourse. In a world focused on immediate results, we will continue to invest in the long-term intellectual, creative, and social potential of our students, faculty, and staff.

The resulting gestalt begins to resemble our collective ambition in which the whole is greater than the sum of the parts. Between *The Brown Difference* and *The Brown Approach*, the tendency is to believe that Brown University is a place that strives to be a different type of Research University.

Finally, there is the need to establish authenticity. The University of Delaware is one of the few Research Universities that gives any indication that their values are part of a process. The institution's strategic plan, *Path to Prominence*, identifies a set of "Guiding Principles."

Five principles, identified during the 2008 planning process, continue to guide our progress. They are at the core of the University's mission and

inspire a commitment to addressing the grand challenges of our time. All members of the University community align their efforts and contextualize their work to support our guiding principles.

❖ ❖ ❖

In general, Research Universities struggle when it comes to describing and communicating what they believe. The key tendency is to, seemingly, just get something down on paper. For example, values appear to be almost an afterthought at the University of Kansas.

The university is committed to excellence. It fosters a multicultural environment in which the dignity and rights of the individual are respected. Intellectual diversity, integrity, and disciplined inquiry in the search for knowledge are of paramount importance.

There simply isn't much here to help guide the institution and the individuals with their daily decisions. That doesn't mean it can't be done.

A fascinating example of "weave values into everything" is offered by the University of California, Berkeley. In the job postings section of Berkeley's website, they begin with an "About Berkeley" statement. The final sentence in that section reads as follows:

In deciding whether to apply for a staff position at Berkeley, candidates are strongly encouraged to consider the alignment of the Berkeley Workplace Culture with their potential for success at http://jobs.berkeley.edu/why-berkeley.html

---

The link takes the prospective employee to another page that is entitled, "Our Workplace Culture:"

As employees of Berkeley, we are part of an institution that uncovers new knowledge, conducts groundbreaking research and shifts the global conversation every single day.

We all do different things. (Very different things.)

But together, we are serving a university that's unlike any other. No matter our role, we help Berkeley redefine what's possible.

We do this by being inclusive—of ideas, of people, of points of view.

By being accountable—to each other, to our teams, to our commitments.

By simplifying whenever possible. (It's often how the best solutions arise.) By taking risks. (And learning from them.) And by serving Berkeley, and everyone who is a part of it, with respect.

Individually, we are experts at what we do. Collectively, our impact is even greater.

As employees of Berkeley, when we reimagine the possibilities of our own world, we shape the one around us.

This is an extraordinary illustration of an institution that is using its culture and values to shape its future. It is literally saying to people, before you hit the "Apply" button please understand that this isn't just about a job and a paycheck. This is about something greater than that.

This is a unique place. Not everyone will fit in. So, think about whether your personal values align with what we believe *before* you apply for a job here.

Master's Colleges and Universities

Most of the institutions in this institutional type stick close to the language of "Values." There are few exceptions. Chapman University speaks to its "Central Commitments" and Appalachian State University uses the term "Essential Character" but, for the most part, these colleges and universities don't seem too interested in developing a unique interpretation on the question, "What do we believe?"

The challenge for this institutional type is similar to what was discussed in the previous chapter on Vision. The tendency is for these institutions to get caught in the middle. They can't speak to a bucolic campus setting and small class sizes. It is difficult to reinforce the idea of "community" with expansive parking lots, commuting students, and large numbers of part-time faculty. At the other end, they don't have the ability to describe their research prowess, global impact, and their Nobel prize-winning faculty members. The challenge extends to the discussion of their values.

The application of the first evaluative criterion (discreteness) to Master's Colleges and Universities largely generated lists—that is, the name of the value but not much else. One interesting result, however, was the use of a gerund or verb at several institutions in order to create meaningfulness. Wilkes University enumerates a set of five values that flow from "Our Mission," "Our Vision," and then "Our Values." The use of gerunds helps to make the beliefs actionable:

- ***Mentorship: Nurturing individuals to understand and act on their abilities while challenging them to achieve great things.***
- ***Scholarship: Advancing knowledge through discovery and research to better educate our constituents.***

- ***Diversity:** Embracing differences and uniqueness through sincerity, awareness, inclusion and sensitivity.*
- ***Innovation:** Promoting creative scholarly activities, programs, ideas and sustainable practices.*
- ***Community:** Appreciating and collaborating with mutual respect to foster a sense of belonging*

Framingham State University does something similar. Each of its six values is immediately followed by a clarifying statement that begins with a verb that implies action. For example:

***Personal and Professional Growth* (note: name of value)—*We aspire to create a nurturing culture where all thrive and are supported in their own paths toward lifelong growth and leadership in personal and professional ways* (note: clarifying statement).**

***Inclusive and Collaborative Community* (note: name of value)—*We seek to encourage a supportive, diverse, collaborative, and cohesive environment in which we learn from each other through informed, clear, and open communication* (note: clarifying statement).**

As with Research Universities, there is a disturbing tendency with this institutional type to generate lists of values that are not meaningful. For example, how meaningful can Bloomsburg University's "Values Statement" be when its beliefs are a set of ten bullets?:"

Collaboration ● Community ● Critical Thinking ● Diversity ● Excellence ● Integrity ● Knowledge ● Opportunity ● Personal and Professional Growth ● Respect

---

There are some important exceptions, though. Rider University has a "Statement of Community Values" that is refreshing in how it describes what it believes to be important:

In our endeavor to make Rider University a just community, we commit ourselves, as caring individuals, to the following principles:

- ***that our rigorous intellectual life nourishes our minds and spirits***
- ***that no person roams these halls as a stranger***
- ***that integrity of word and deed forms the foundation of all relationships***
- ***that we recognize that real leadership is derived from service to others***
- ***that we celebrate our differences for they are our strength***
- ***that we are proud of this special place, entrusted to us by past generations, nurtured by us for future ones***
- ***that we share not one Truth, but respect our common pursuit for understanding***
- ***and through the time we spend here, we are forever joined to each other and to Rider University***

Appalachian State University's mission was described in Chapter Three. It begins: "Appalachian State University prepares students to lead purposeful lives as engaged global citizens who understand their responsibilities in creating a sustainable future for all." This focus on sustainability provides a distinctive purpose which, in turn, is reinforced by their statement of "Essential Character and Core Values:"

Appalachian State University is located in the Blue Ridge Mountains, a place of great beauty and cultural and recreational opportunity. The mountains inspire an appreciation for the traditions of the region as we connect to and learn from the world. We are a teaching institution with small classes in an innovative, interdisciplinary, and integrative curriculum

> ***supported by a faculty dedicated to research and invested in new strategies and technologies. Our faculty and staff inspire our students, who have a strong service ethic and involvement in the community. The green ethos at Appalachian infuses academic programs, environmental stewardship, research, and a community with an attitude of care for the planet.***

The process that is used to reveal what matters most to individuals is what makes values authentic as does being intentional about how those beliefs are manifested in the everyday lives of individuals.

Bentley University provides an illustration of how authenticity can help influence the development and communication of values. It sends a message to stakeholders that the institution has taken the time to reflect on what it believes. And Bentley doesn't shy away from this task. It even goes so far as to couch the language in terms of accepting responsibility for shaping a culture. This approach stands in stark contrast to what others seem to see as a chore: We have a mission statement, a vision, and now we need a set of values.

The Bentley Beliefs

> ***Bentley University is a community of faculty, students and staff who are gathered to learn and to support learning. To maintain and nurture our community and to maximize learning, we embrace the Bentley Beliefs, which govern our conduct in classrooms, residence halls, and places of work. Our learning is a privilege. It is predicated upon our acceptance of the responsibilities described below.***

Moreover, the institution attempts to extend that authenticity to how it describes the individual beliefs. As an example, the first value is "respect." But in addition to naming it, the institution has extended the description in a way that reveals what that means at Bentley:

We strive at all times to treat each other with respect.

In language, personal interactions, and the treatment of property not our own, we treat others as they would like to be treated. We recognize the inherent dignity and worth of every person in our community. We are each responsible to help keep our community safe, without vandalism, hate speech, physical violence, and harassment.

As noted in this and previous chapters, Master's Colleges and Universities face a unique caught-in-the-middle challenge. Many of the institutions seek to reach higher. They believe they need to develop strong graduate programs and even offer doctoral degrees. Others use language that reflects a global perspective. Still others work hard to craft a vision of an institution that cares deeply about students and student success. They take a more personal perspective.

Finally, we should return to the important directive stated at the beginning of this chapter—"Weave core values into everything." Not many institutions take this prescription seriously. Drake University does. Its "Statement of Values" begins with a few sentences that make it very clear that Drake is serious about weaving core values into everything they do:

Drake University's mission, vision, ongoing operations, and strategic planning are all informed by a set of core values that, in essence, define who we are—and what we want to be—as a University. It is critical that these values guide us in the small choices that we make on a daily basis, and in the large choices that we make in crafting the future of the institution—these values determine what we do and how we do it.

Values Summary

A mission statement delineates a clear and specific description of an organization's fundamental purpose. A vision statement presents what the organization wants to become and gives direction for its future. Values clarify how individuals within the organization will conduct themselves on a daily basis in order to honor the mission and achieve a vision. As the third and final part of the principle elements of a collective ambition, values are the most personal and relevant to our every-day professional lives.

After all, a mission is a written document that has been carefully constructed to meet an accreditation standard and provide guidance on a whole range of choices—in our case, what programs and services to offer, what degrees to confer, what markets to serve, and so on. A vision is an idea about a desired state. It is most effective when individuals' personal visions align with a stated vision for the organizational whole and provides a basis for institutional advancement.

But values are about person-to-person relationships that affect everything we do and everyone we do it with. They are ever present. They help guide every decision that an individual makes.

So, it is disappointing to find that only about one-third of the studied institutions had an easily accessible mission, vision, *and* values. This result is particularly vexing because institutions of higher education generally think of themselves as being organizations that have a greater sense of community than, for instance, a corporation. Indeed, article after article, speech after speech, book after book, bemoan the commodification of higher education. We are horrified with the thought that students should be treated as customers. We push back hard when programs, classes, and practices cross the line from "education" to "training." We bemoan the fact that there is a bottom-line (budget) other than learning and the transference of knowledge.

And yet we seem reluctant to capture our specialness in a set of deeply-held beliefs that can help guide behaviors such as UC Berkeley's "Workplace Culture" or Brown University's "Brown Approach."

❖ ❖ ❖

The development of values should happen in a composed and thoughtful environment. We should take the time to reflect on what matters most and how to communicate those values when the seas are relatively calm. Unfortunately, the tendency is to wait until gale force winds are upon us, when the seas have turned rough and unpredictable, to react to specific, unfortunate events. The case of Steven Salaita and University of Illinois at Urbana-Champaign is illustrative.

Steven Salaita, a professor at Virginia Tech, was offered a tenured professorship in American Indian Studies at the University of Illinois at Urbana-Champaign. Before he could arrive on campus, however, the Chancellor notified him that the Board had decided to revoke the written offer. It happened that Mr. Salaita had a colorful and controversial past with particular concern for using obscenities and vitriolic language in denouncing Israel's military action in Gaza. His use of social media was both prolific and provocative.

The uproar was immediate and provoked threats of a boycott against the institution, votes of no confidence against the Chancellor, the involvement of the American Association of University Professors, and dozens of articles each followed by a long list of comments. According to many, this was a direct and scurrilous attack on academic freedom, a core value of virtually every institution of higher education in the country.

At some point, the Chancellor was obliged to send an open letter to the campus explaining the decision. After promising her full support "to welcome and encourage differing perspectives," she went on to say:

"What we cannot and will not tolerate at the University of Illinois are personal and disrespectful words or actions that demean and abuse

either viewpoints themselves or those we express them. We have a particular duty to our students to ensure that they live in a community of scholarship that challenges their assumptions about the world but also respects their rights as individuals."

The Chancellor then added her personal view:

"As Chancellor, it is my responsibility to ensure that all perspectives are welcome and that our discourse, regardless of subject matter or viewpoint, allows new concepts and differing points of view to be discussed in and outside the classroom in a scholarly, civil and productive manner."

The pushback against this call for "civility" came from those who felt that university administrators were using the value as a means of silencing and getting rid of professors deemed politically troublesome. On the other hand, the Chancellor's concerns were reinforced by the "2015 Survey of College and University Chief Academic Officers" from *Inside Higher Ed* that concluded the following:

- **Almost three-quarters of Chief Academic Officers (CAOs) are very or somewhat concerned about declining civility among higher education faculty.**
- **CAOs indicate that professors are likelier to treat students civilly than they are to treat their faculty peers or administrators that way.**
- **More than 8 in 10 CAOs agree or strongly agree that civility should be a criterion for evaluating performance.**

How does all of this square with the institution? What does this mean for the university and the individuals to have and communicate a shared set of beliefs as part of their collective ambition? Illinois's website has all the bells and whistles of other Research Universities: Large tiles with striking pictures under "Athletics," "Research," "Campus Life," "Illinois in the News," and others. Then there is "About." On the left navigation bar are the following headings:

Overview* ● *Leadership* ● *Research Milestones* ● *Nobels and Pulitzers* ● *Rankings* ● *Campus Tours

---

Under the "Overview" tab is, among other things, a mission and vision. There are no values in sight. But a search for the strategic plan found a *pdf* of *University of Illinois at Urbana-Champaign (2013-16)* that has a set of 14 "Guiding Principles" including, "We will focus and broaden our fundraising efforts to inspire donors and funders to support our highest institutional priorities."

There is nothing about civility. So, raising funds is a guiding principle but how people treat each other is not?

This specific illustration brings us full circle. Values shouldn't be an afterthought or a list of words on a page buried in a document. They aren't just the result of someone saying, "We need to generate some values to go along with our mission and vision statements." We shouldn't be invoking a value after-the-fact in order to justify a tough decision. Instead, our beliefs are the perfect and critical complement to mission and vision because they are (or should be) carried around every day in people's hearts.

Questions to Ask

As with mission and vision, a series of "values questions" need to be asked:

Looking Back

- What was the process used to identify your current set of values?
- Why do you think it was done that way?

The Current Situation

- If your institution doesn't have a set of stated values, why do you think that is so?
- If you were to ask a broad range of stakeholders about the institution believes, what language would they use?

Looking Forward

- What values best align with your current mission statement?
- What values will need to be present in the institution for your vision to become reality?
- What fundamental beliefs are prized within the institution?
- Are these principles explicit or implicit?
- Does the understanding permeate the organization?
- How can the institution ensure that the values are lived every day?

6

Promising Practices

The nature of a *Fieldbook* was described in the Introduction. This book, like Senge's *The Fifth Discipline Fieldbook*, is designed to answer the question, "What should we do on Monday morning?" To that end, a critical examination of 141 colleges and universities was undertaken to provide the answer. In a hyperactive environment with engaged stakeholders, the idea has been to help institutions take responsibility for their own tomorrow by making better, more informed decisions.

The Socratic Approach yielded a set of follow-on questions: Why do we exist?, What do we want to create?, and What do we believe? And the analyses of the answers to those questions by institutional types and by evaluative criteria resulted in a detailed enumeration of institutional examples throughout the three corresponding chapters. The "Questions to Ask" section at the end of each of the mission, vision, and values chapters then allows institutions and groups of individuals to reflect on how to be intentional about their own future—their *Future College*.

This final chapter takes a different turn.

Pulling back from a granular look at specific text and terms at particular institutions reveals a sweep of ideas that are common to all colleges and universities. These "Promising Practices" are important because they give institutions the ability to make more reasoned decisions on how to move forward—or which way to go.

Again, too often, these discussions occur in a vacuum. Mission, vision, and values are derived from a small group of well-intentioned individuals who are looking inward, relying on their professional

experiences and personal feelings, without the benefit of having studied what has proven to be effective at other institutions.

It is also important to note that these practices are informed by and expand on a series of recommendations described by the author in *Noble Ambitions: Mission, Vision, and Values in American Community Colleges* (2013). That critical examination followed a similar methodology but focused more narrowly on the largest segment of higher education: community colleges.

Nine Promising Practices intended to help operationalize *Future College* are organized into three sets of three.

The first set reflects approaches that might be used as an institution begins to think about the manner and means of addressing its collective ambition. They are foundational and apply broadly to the other practices:

1. Time on Task
2. Language Matters
3. Process Matters, Too

The next set of three promising practices focuses individually on mission, vision, and values:

4. Be on a Mission
5. Search for Distinctiveness
6. Hypocrisy Kills

The final three practices are concerned with what should happen when deciding how to implement a more purposeful approach to direction setting:

7. Keep Folding Things In
8. Don't Bury the Lead
9. How are we Doing?

Time on Task

Many people are familiar with the famous Lucille Ball sketch of Lucy and Ethel in the wrapping department at a candy factory. As the belt speeds up they resort to eating the candy, then stuffing candy into their hats and blouses. No matter what they do they can't keep up. It must feel that way with our colleges and universities. More and more demands have been layered on us but resources have remained scarce. The things we have to do have squeezed out all the things we'd like to do. E-mails keep coming. Meetings keep coming. Reports keep coming. Each crisis is barely contained before the next one bursts on the scene.

At the same time, research in decision sciences is quite clear. We are able, as individuals, to instinctively generate "to-do" lists in our brains. We know what is most important and what is least important. We also know that those things that are most important are those that are the most complex and difficult to complete. In contrast, the simple tasks tend to be the least important—like e-mails, phone calls, and meetings. And we go home exhausted—like Lucy and Ethel—by all the hard work we did that day.

But what we have done, often unknowingly, is to attack the bottom of the list (those things that won't make much difference anyway) while letting the larger, challenging issues remain untouched and unsolved. The resulting "immediacy versus reflection" dialectic has been a part of philosophy since the Danish philosopher Kierkegaard. But it doesn't require us to delve through the approaches described by a 19th philosopher and others to understand this phenomenon. We all do this. We are "immediate men."

The data and analyses provided in the chapters on mission, vision, and values reinforce this idea. Mission statements do not appear to be the result of extended, productive conversations; visions are not generally compelling and certainly not shared; and values are too often lists of individual words with no clarifying statements and no behavioral attributes.

Why is this so?

Colleges and universities are filled with very smart and deeply caring individuals. So, we cannot conclude that these results are a function of institutional indifference. The conclusion must be that too many of us are simply overwhelmed by immediate concerns such that the topics of purpose, future, and beliefs—the really, really important questions—never get full and considered attention.

The remedy, the promising practice, is to devote more time and energy to the fundamental questions that should drive the institution.

"Time on task" is certainly not a foreign concept to educators. It has been one of the most widely-discussed concepts among educational researchers since the 1970s beginning with John Carroll's 1963 paper, "A Model of School Learning," which directly linked learning to time. Perhaps the best example of this in higher education is the classic "Seven Principles of Good Practice in Undergraduate Education" as originally developed by Art Chickering and Zelda Gamson (1991). One of the seven principles, "Time on Task," states the following:

"Time plus energy equals learning. There is no substitute for time on task. Learning to use one's time well is critical for students and professionals alike. Students need help in learning effective time management. Allocating realistic amounts of time means effective learning for students and effective teaching for faculty. How an institution defines time expectations for students, faculty, administrators, and other professional staff can establish the basis for high performance for all."

So, as an organization that seeks to learn, to thrive, and to involve lots of people in continuous improvement, it follows that colleges and universities need to spend more time on those things that matter most. More time on the question, "Why do we exist?" more time on the question, "What do we want to create?" and more time on the question, "What do we believe?" This needs to be high-quality focused time, with engaged groups, who are willing to apply the kind of evaluative criteria developed in this *Fieldbook* to their own situation.

It should also be noted that "time on task" is important not just when developing our collective ambition but also the time devoted to reflecting on the choices made. One of the defining characteristics of "reflective practice," as defined by Donald Schon (1987) is "the capacity to reflect on action so as to engage in a process of continuous learning." This practice-based learning is a function of professionals gaining development insight from their own experiences, rather than from formal teaching or knowledge transfer. In education, reflective practice often refers narrowly to the process of professors studying their own teaching methods and determining what works best for the students. More generally, though, faculty, staff and administrators should be studying their institution, as professionals, to determine what is working, what is not, and how that relates to their stated ambitions.

In summary, this promising practice first involves carving out enough time from fighting fires to devote to the challenging task of asking and answering very fundamental questions involving the future and then having the courage to reflect on those choices such that necessary positive adjustments can be made.

Georgia Tech University, Kenyon College, and Stetson University are a few of the institutions that have made significant investments of time and energy in helping to create their own futures. Georgia Tech has documented an exhaustive, comprehensive process that includes an advisory group, community input, implementation efforts, timelines and progress reports. Kenyon College has taken a similar "time on task" approach. Their *2020 Strategic Plan* has a "Conversations" page that includes the following statement that shows a commitment to productive conversations around things that matter :

Between October 2013 and March 2014, President Decatur met with alumni, parents and friends of the College in 12 small-group gatherings in cities across the country. On campus he held 11 meetings with faculty, staff and students. All together more than 600 individuals participated in a conversation about Kenyon's future. Out of these discussions three common themes emerged that will serve as the focus of the Kenyon 2020 initiative.

Finally, Stetson University also appears to have found the time to devote to deciding which way to go. First, its planning efforts include a review of previous planning efforts and the results. Next, the current planning process is documented along with the resources used to inform decision-making, and a strategic map is developed. Many of the planning sessions—for example, a President-led visioning retreat—are posted for everyone to see and comment.

These are the kind of productive conversations and reflective practices that are desperately needed in all our colleges and universities.

Language Matters

This is a foundational promising practice that should be obvious to people in higher education. So much of what we do involves defining terms, creating categorization schema, describing in great detail various phenomena, and developing theories that must be tested (and replicated) using precise methods. All of this—and much more—requires that we pay particular attention to the language we use. Indeed, survey courses are largely about communicating the lexicon of an individual discipline so that additional, more advanced work can use that language to create and transfer knowledge.

So, shouldn't we be equally engaged in how we describe our future college?

There are three important aspects to this promising practice. The first is "the basics." It is not a coincidence that each of the core chapters of mission, vision, and values is written with a subhead—an accompanying question. Definitions can often drone on. But the three terms are so critical that a simple question is used to ensure agreement. We need to know that a mission statement is fundamentally the answer to the question, "Why do we exist?" When a vision is followed up with the question "What we want to create?" it becomes apparent that it is quite different from what is in a mission statement. And when we ask "What do we believe?" it further differentiates another element of how we might describe our future.

Throughout earlier chapters it was noted that the search for mission, vision, and values was hampered at times because of the creative combinations and interpretations. Missions were sometimes folded under a heading "History." Other times a mission read more like a vision or the terms were simply used interchangeably.

In general, the critical examination of this work was often hampered by the inability to understand exactly what the institutions meant by the terms they used. Without definitions in place, the language tended to wander and meaning became difficult to nail down. Indeed, it was a challenge to believe that some institutions really understood the true meaning of their own mission, vision and values statements.

Perhaps the best advice here is to pull a page from one of evaluative criteria used in the Values chapter—"a clarifying statement that defines the terms." A few examples are useful. The College of Wooster had a "Vision Statement" that begins "Our collective endeavor . . ." Their "Core Values" begin "These are the values that govern our shared pursuits, the idea that we hold true . . ." The obvious idea is to not assume that everyone—including the work teams who are drafting the materials—have a common understanding of mission, vision, and values and how they interrelate.

A second aspect of this promising practice is stated in the negative—"don't be lazy." The critical examination revealed an abundance of the use of words such as "excellence" and "quality." Such words lack meaningfulness. They are used so often and with such alacrity that they seem adopted as short hand for the tough work that is required when striving to be distinctive. At other times the language being used is seemingly a tumble of words that manifest themselves as clichés—things that the institutions believe they should be saying about themselves. The exercise at the end of Chapter Four (Vision) in which the institutions and vision statements were so generic as to be interchangeable is illustrative.

The language that an institution uses to describe itself—and its preferred future—can help differentiate it from many other institutions with similar missions. Appalachian State University is such a unique place. It was noted in Chapter Three (Mission) that their mission begins, "Our location in the distinctive Appalachian mountain town of Boone, North Carolina, profoundly shapes who we are." And distinctive language is used throughout. For example, the "Essential Character and Core Values" section ends with, "The green ethos at Appalachian infuses academic programs, environmental stewardship, research, and a community with an attitude of care for the planet." No one can accuse the institution of being lazy with their language.

Finally, it important to consider the notion that often we need to "say more with less." It was noted in both the Mission and Vision chapters that some statements were exceedingly long. As any writer will tell you, it is usually more difficult to be concise with language than to pile words together resulting in what appears to be a stream of consciousness exercise. In general, parsimony pays. It pays because the reader doesn't get lost in the language and comes away with a feeling that the institution thoughtfully labored over each and every word.

This promising practice aligns with the core concept of emotional contagion. Language can be used to create the kind of lift that is needed to engage and excite individuals. Aspirational language is able to paint a picture of where the institution needs to be in the future and how individuals need to treat each other. By comparing that hopeful tomorrow with the reality of today, structural tension (divine discontent) surfaces. Resolution is sought and a bias for action results. Lycoming College captures this need to describe a desired state when they complete their vision with the following sentence: "To achieve this vision, we must harness our energies and inspire our supporters and, most importantly, exercise our collective imaginations to build an even Greater Lycoming." Indeed, language can help exercise an institution's collective imagination and bring it to life— an even Greater Lycoming.

Process Matters, Too

The final foundational practice is fairly straightforward. The answer to the "Why do we exist?" question is not simply a mission statement that appears in a catalogue. A vision isn't a future that emerges whole cloth from a retreat. Institutional values don't just materialize and they certainly don't automatically translate into deeply-held personal beliefs.

The best mission, vision, and value statements are ultimately only as good as the processes that are used to develop, communicate, implement, and evaluate them.

Where we get into trouble is when we see these statements as events. Indeed, we can go back even further in this book to our Core Concepts. A "collective ambition" involves a set of relationships—purpose, vision, milestones, strategic priorities, and so on—that interact in a particular way to create movement. The development of "structural tension" involves a series of steps that create a discrepancy which ultimately results in resolution. "Emotional contagion" is the psychological lift that occur when self-efficacy becomes real to people and "constancy of purpose" is when all of these concepts—working together—dominate the effort put forth by individuals for a new and different future. These are not individual occurrences. They are courses of action.

Many organizational development models are, in effect, process models. For example, the most well-known such model is the Baldrige Performance Excellence Program which was first awarded in 1988 through the Department of Commerce. It now has four distinct programs: business, health care, education, and nonprofit. The purpose of the education framework is to help an organization answer three questions: Is your organization doing as well as it could?

How do you know? What and how should your organization improve or change? It does this by asking questions that represent seven critical aspects of managing and performing as an organization (divided into six interrelated process categories and a results category).

Importantly, the framework emphasizes "a focus on processes:"

Processes are the methods your organization uses to accomplish its work. The Baldrige framework helps you assess and improve your processes along four dimensions:

1. ***Approach: designing and selecting effective processes, methods, and measures.***
2. ***Deployment: implementing your approach consistently across the organization.***
3. ***Learning: assessing your progress and capturing new knowledge, including looking for opportunities for improvement and innovation.***
4. ***Integration: aligning your approach with your organization's needs; ensuring that your measures, information, and improvement systems complement each other across processes and work units; and harmonizing processes and operations across your organization to achieve key organization-wide goals.***

A similar type of process model has been used extensively in higher education. In *Once Upon a Campus: Lesson for Improving Quality and Productivity in Higher Education* (1995), the author proposed a Performance Improvement Framework. It began with a "Direction Setting" component and has a series of lessons associated with "Enablers" that involve leadership and a systems view. It has a "Feedback" component that seeks to describe the mechanics of continuous improvement and organizational learning. But the focus of the framework is a set of four lessons associated with "Process Design and Management."

So, how should "process" be used to help advance a college's ambition? When developing mission, vision, and values statements and aligning them with a strategic planning effort it is critical to keep four general process components in place: inclusion, transparency, feedback, and documentation. Inclusion is the obvious starting point. It is always important, especially in a college with all its nooks and crannies, to begin with broad, representative teams that provide necessary perspective. While everyone doesn't need to be at the table, all stakeholder groups need to have an opportunity to share their ideas. This can be done through focus groups, visioning sessions, surveys, and so on.

Next, the processes need to be abundantly transparent. Communicate the approach being used, do it again, and then do it some more. Find every venue and occasion to talk about the efforts being put in to creating the institution's future. Use the website, intranet, and collaborative software to describe the process and draft results as they are emerging.

The next element, feedback, is used to expand the circle of engagement beyond the immediate teams by posting draft materials and asking for suggestions. The key is to ask for input because the process needs to be iterative. Again, as just noted, these processes need to be inclusive—so, if everyone can't be at the table that doesn't mean that everyone shouldn't have the opportunity to comment on draft materials. By doing so, people have a stake in the end product. And it is also critical to see mission, vision, and values through the lens of continuous improvement. There is always a better way. That is why the question, "How will we know if we are successful?" needs to be asked over and over again.

Finally, all this work needs to be documented. That is why more and more institutions are turning to a different organizational structure such that a senior administrator is responsible for institutional effectiveness (including strategic planning, institutional research, and other functions). Without such ownership, things are just done and the appropriate boxes are ticked. But there is no sense of history or causality—that is, the ability to connect means and ends and then codify the processes.

❖ ❖ ❖

In the General Findings chapter it was noted that far too often missions, visions, and even values were found tucked away under a heading "Administration," "University Leadership," "President" or some other related banner. It should be evident now why that result was so disturbing. The implication is that someone or a small group was responsible for future of the institution. The lack of implementation plans, widespread communications efforts, well-documented evaluative measures, and very few institutional effectiveness models tends to reduce buy-in and undermine the concept of constancy of purpose.

You get a very different sense when reviewing Lewis and Clark College's strategic plan for 2020—*The Journey Forward.* The Appendix begins with a section entitled "Who Mapped Our Journey Forward:"

Many people from across the College community contributed to the plan articulated in this document. Over the course of summer and early fall 2011 a task force devoted hours to identifying cross-school strengths that could form the focus of an institution-wide strategic plan. Beginning in the late fall of 2011 and continuing to May 2012 strategic planning work groups addressed each of the priorities identified by the task force. They gathered insight from the wider community regarding their assigned topics; discussed and identified appropriate goals to move the College forward on their priority; and made recommendations for concrete actions to be taken going forward. Overseeing this process was a small steering committee. Unnamed below, but deeply significant to creating this report are also the many others on campus who contributed their views and opinions, data and information, wisdom and insight. To all—those named and unnamed—we extend our gratitude for their insights and service.

The sense is that the institution's journey forward is indeed a journey and that many individuals and groups are contributing to that future.

Be on a Mission

There is a huge difference between having a mission statement (as per an accreditation standard) and creating a sense of movement—*being on a mission.* The standards enumerated by accrediting associations (Appendix B) were used to create a set of evaluative criteria used in Chapter Three. Nonetheless, there is a tendency to see mission statements in terms of business value-added. You have to have one. But the core purpose of an institution should be about adding value by giving individuals a sense of meaning.

And all of that begins with *Why?*

The essence of this promising practice is described by Simon Sinek in his popular book *Start with Why: How Great Leaders Inspire Everyone to take Action* (2011). Sinek uses his Golden Circle to explain. The outer ring is WHAT. It describes an organization's products or services. As such, WHATs are easy to identify. The next ring is HOW. These are the factors that motivate or even differentiate the products or services. They are more difficult to describe. The inner circle, the core, is WHY. This is purpose, cause, or belief. Or as Sinek says, "WHY do you get out of bed in the every morning? And WHY should anyone care?" When most organizations or people think or act they do so from the outside in, from WHAT to WHY. The primary reason is because the clearest thing, the easiest to comprehend, is the WHAT. The fuzziest thing, the most difficult to define, is at the core—the WHY.

Colleges and universities are largely concerned with WHAT. Remember those jam-packed websites described in General Findings? There are athletics and campus maps. There are photo tours and the mascot. Information is available about programs of study, class schedules, and the academic calendar. Most colleges, even small ones, have hundreds of classes and dozens upon dozens of programs. That is a lot of product to push.

Then there is the HOW. We have to get our students admitted, counseled, registered, and there are financial arrangements to be concluded.

That is a lot of WHAT and HOW. But what about the WHY? Sinek argues that WHY is the primary and most powerful motivator of human behavior but then explains that most organizations—as we have just seen—don't start there. They start with and stick with WHAT and HOW.

When you reverse the order an entirely different dynamic is in play. He uses the example of Apple. A marketing message from Apple, if they were to sound like everyone else, might sound like the following:

We make great computers.

They're beautifully designed, simple to use and user-friendly

Wanna buy one?

This approach focuses on products and features much like a college or university pitching programs and a schedule that has evening and on-line classes. But what happens when the hard work and deep digging of WHY is the starting point? How did that allow Apple to develop such brand loyalty and universal respect for its operations? This time, the example starts with WHY:

Everything we do, we believe in challenging the status quo. We believe in thinking differently.

The way we challenge the status quo is by making our products beautifully designed, simple to use and user-friendly.

And we happen to make great computers.

Wanna buy one?

A mission statement should, fundamentally, be about WHY—"Why do we exist?" Yes, it is the one element of an ambition that is

universally required. But it is also the one element that gets to the very soul of the operation of the institution. Indeed, if you can't get the purpose question right, the other questions don't really matter much.

❖ ❖ ❖

The core concept of structural tension is important here. Again, the discrepancy between a desired state and an actual state creates discrepancy or the idea of structural tension. This is a call to action such that the discrepancy is resolved.

University of Central Oklahoma provides an illustration. An early indication is the page titled, "Mission, Vision & Call to Action." The Strategy Statement speaks to Transformative Learning and then goes to issue a Call to Action:

The University of Central Oklahoma is the Leadership University, delivering education based on our shared values of Community, Character and Civility. UCO transforms each student by focusing our resources on the Central Six tenets of transformative learning:

- ***All students will be transformed with:***
- ***Discipline Knowledge***
- ***Leadership***
- ***Problem Solving (Research, Scholarly and Creative Activities***
- ***Service Learning and Civic Engagement***
- ***Global and Cultural Competencies***
- ***Health and Wellness***

Transformative learning is a holistic process that places students at the center of their own active and reflective learning experience.

The Strategic Plan, *Vision 2020,* goes on to identify teams of faculty, staff and administrators organized into four strategic directions and charged with recommending annual operational plans that establish objectives and recommend priorities on budgetary allocations. The strategic directions are: Create a Culture of Collaboration and Change, Redefine Ourselves as Oklahoma's Metropolitan University, Align our Outcomes with Mission and Vision, and Align our Resources to Serve Strategic Stakeholders.

Everything speaks to resolution or the means to reduce structural tension. The language of "Call to Action" and "Transformative Learning" is important. A plan that has such operational elements is an institution doesn't just have a mission but is on a mission.

Search for Distinctiveness

Senge's notion of a "compelling shared vision" suggests that the described future needs to evoke an emotional response among individuals within the organization. It must captivate the imagination. And when it does, when a compelling shared future captures the imagination of individuals, it can be one of most powerful forces on earth.

Sameness is not compelling. Similarity and uniformity do not create any sense of urgency or aspirational drive. Comfort is the natural occurrence when things are predictable. There simply is no lift or emotional contagion when the future is perceived to be no different from the present. Everyone settles in. Objects (and organizations) at rest tend to stay at rest.

A classic illustration of what is possible comes from a very unusual place—a shipbuilding company. Newport News Ship Building was founded in 1886. One hundred years later a book was published, *Always Good Ships*, to document its extraordinary history. The book reflected on what it took for a company to grow over a century and gave much of the credit to its founder, Collis Potter Huntington, and its vision:

We Shall Build Good Ships Here; At A Profit If We Can, At A Loss If We Must, But Always Good Ships.

It is easy to talk about excellence or quality in abstract terms that essentially mean nothing. It is something else to describe it in such a way that it provides a compelling shared vision that lasts a century and beyond. As noted in *Always Good Ships*, Huntington's vision "specified for his shipbuilders in no uncertain terms that there should be no scrimping on the product—profit or loss should be minor considerations as long as Good Ships were the result."

When this illustration is evaluated with the "stickiness" criteria enumerated in Chapter in Four—simplicity, unexpectedness, concreteness, credibility, emotional, stories—the power of the statement should be evident. It is Velcro sticky.

It follows that if a shipbuilding company can describe a commanding future, institutions of higher education should be equally accomplished at describing their "future college." Unfortunately, that is not what this critical examination found. Many of the institutions had vision statements that rambled on and on. The language was often wispy and lacked passion. If anything, much of the language used by institutions was very expected. Baccalaureate Colleges spoke about students and community, Research Universities described their pre-eminence in research and global impact, and Master's College and Universities dwelled on their regional influence and access.

Within institutional types we seem to focus on what we have in common with other institutions, not what differentiates us and makes the college or university a special place. There are certainly aspects of distinctiveness. Moravian College's "a community of the great embrace" and Juniata College's focus on inspiring "citizens of consequence" use intriguing language. There is Georgia Tech's soliloquy that begins with "Imagine an institution that . . ." and a bravely stated future in which a common question in research, business, the media, and government would be, "What does Georgia Tech think?"

But most institutions haven't found a distinctive way to speak to excellence as well as a 19th century shipbuilder managed to do.

❖ ❖ ❖

There is a "compelling shared vision" test for organizations. It doesn't require a complicated research design. A high-powered consulting firm doesn't need to be hired to conduct the test. The human subjects committee doesn't need to be involved nor a task force formed. The test involves a convenience sample of faculty members, staff members, students, and the occasional administrator. This breadth of input is necessary to ensure that "shared" is part of the equation. Next, "compelling" is derived from the answer to a simple question: "What makes this institution special?"

Anyone can administer the test. All you have to do is walk the campus, bump into people, and ask them the question. The hard part—as with all qualitative research—is to listen intently to the responses. You are interested in the language, the specific words and phrases that individuals use to describe their surroundings and their aspirations. You are looking for patterns—that is, lots and lots of people using the same distinctive language to describe the institution. The compelling part will come from the energy, enthusiasm, and uniqueness around the words and phrases being used. It should become quickly evident that the language wouldn't apply to the organization down the street or even the college on the other side of town.

There shouldn't be a lot of generic terms being used. Having "excellent" faculty or mentioning some "quality" program programs is not enough. Any college or university can say that. Indeed, most of them do. So it follows that most college or university visions for the future are eminently forgettable because there is nothing to inspire.

Being special is really daring to be different and then building on it. As such, it is an act of courage.

Hypocrisy Kills

One of the more fascinating expositions on values was written by Benjamin Franklin. *The Means and Manner of Obtaining Virtue* first details a set of values that Franklin deemed to be important and then a process by which he sought to live those values every day. Today, most people believe that values are important. There certainly seems to be a lot of talk about values—family values, progressive values. Judeo-Christian values—and many organizations like to stress their values-driven nature.

While this critical examination struggled at times to find an institution's values statement on their website or in a catalogue, it is nonetheless clear that most of them perceive themselves to be concerned about their beliefs—"Our Core Values," "Guiding Principles," "Central Commitments," and so on.

The intriguing thing about Franklin's exposition is the "means and manner." He detailed a system in which he focused on one value for a month. After he had cycled through all 13 of them he started at the beginning again. His system was designed to move beyond espousing virtuousness to being intentional about becoming more virtuous.

Why is this important?

Fast forward a couple of hundred years to another classic book—*What we say/What we do* by Irwin Deutscher (1973). The author, a sociologist, reviewed and analyzed dozens of experiments in which people were asked about something such as their views about drinking or racial attitudes. Then, the experimenters watched their behaviors. The evidence is disturbing: people often do not do what they say and may sometimes do just the opposite, leading Deutscher to conclude, "If we could not count on what people told us, then we had to be much more attentive to what they were doing." What happens in an organizational setting when what we say doesn't match what we do? What happens when the values we espouse as an institution aren't reflected in individuals' actions?

First, understand that all the people at your college or university are watching and listening. Throughout the day, in meetings and in memos, at events and in the hallways, the leadership of an institution is showing what it values. How they interact, how they behave, and how they invest their most scarce resource—their time—reflects who they are and what they believe in. Faculty members, secretaries, groundskeepers, registration clerks, and others pick up on the cues—intended and unintended, big and small.

They do not miss much . . . and then they talk among themselves. Any discrepancy between what you say and what you do will be apparent to them. And the resulting hypocrisy will, over time, slowly erode trust in the individuals and then the organization as a whole.

That is why the behavioral attributes of a value are so critical. They make values tangible such that what we say can be made intentional (like Franklin) and match what we do.

❖ ❖ ❖

An illustration is useful. Youngstown State University has a strategic plan—*YSU 2020*. The plan begins with mission and vision and then adds that the vision will be supported by a set of core values: centrality of students, excellence and innovation, integrity/human dignity, and collegiality and public engagement. It goes on to state that:

In addition to the core values stated earlier, YSU is committed to two over-arching principles that can be seen in each of the four cornerstones and that must guide each of the University's activities and initiatives:

- ***Commitment to diversity and inclusiveness, in the broadest sense, and***
- ***Commitment to 'continuous quality improvement,' or a 'culture of assessment.'***

The problem is that the University's strategic planning page features a link to "For the most recent progress report." The plan began in 2011 and there is a 2012 update. And then there is nothing. So, while one of only two guiding principles that "must guide each of the University's activities and initiatives" is a commitment to continuous quality improvement, there is no (obvious) evidence that any feedback—the core of continuous improvement—is being developed, used, and communicated. There really doesn't appear to be a "culture of assessment."

This is hypocrisy—*saying one thing and doing something else*—and it will, over time, kill any effort to use core values as the means to engage people in creating their own future.

Folding Things In

The first promising practice associated with implementing mission, vision, and values involves alignment. The tendency in higher education organizations is for different units, divisions, departments to "do their own thing." This is what loosely-coupled systems do. They tend to be less interdependent with less coordination and less information flow. The problem, as has been stated, is that loose-coupling is much more effective when the environment is stable. In a high velocity environment there is a need to be more responsive to shifts and swings in stakeholder demands and political, economic, social, and technological trends.

There are several useful metaphors to describe what needs to happen. Peter Senge (cited in this and earlier chapters) uses a large arrow and a set of smaller ones to illustrate the concept of alignment. The large arrow represents the purpose, the vision of the organization. Within that large arrow, smaller arrows denote the interests and actions of individuals within the organization. In the first graphic, an illustration of an unaligned institution, the individual arrows are shooting off in all different directions. Some are even punching through the back of the big arrow headed in the opposite direction. "The fundamental characteristic of the relatively unaligned team is wasted energy," notes Senge. By contrast, when a team becomes more aligned, a commonality of interests and direction emerges. There is less wasted energy. Indeed, as is readily apparent from the second graphic, when the arrows all align, there is a synergy of individual interests that begin to complement and reinforce one another.

For a college or university what this is suggesting is that the mission, vision, and values should be the beginning, not the end, of the conversation. Every day, hundreds of decisions are made by hundreds of individuals on everything from which courses and programs to offer to how financial aid disbursements are made. Those decisions require investments of time, energy, and money. As such, our collective ambition can and should act as a guide for decision-makers. Indeed, it is not far-fetched to suggest that for every major decision that is made, a mental checklist should be used:

- Does this decision support our stated purpose?
- Does this decision help us to fulfill our desired future?
- Does this decision reflect how we have agreed to treat each other?

A second metaphor used in *Noble Ambitions* is the idea "folding things in." Anyone who has spent any time in the kitchen is familiar with the technique. Two or more ingredients are brought together and, usually using a rubber spatula or wooden spoon, they are blended together using a light, gentle motion. The exercise is not as aggressive as mixing. Think of the mission, vision, and values of an institution as the main ingredients. Everything else, all the programs, policies or personnel decisions for example, need to be made in the context of whether or not they can be "folded in." After all, the institution ultimately operates as a whole, so the question should always come back to whether or not the new ingredient is compatible with the other key ingredients.

Regardless of whether you use the image of arrows being aligned, or ingredients being folded into recipes, this promising practice is focused on becoming intentional about the use of purpose, aspirations and beliefs in making day-to-day decisions about the operations of your institution.

❖ ❖ ❖

It was noted in the Introduction that the two best times to reflect on a college or university's future is as part of the accreditation process or the strategic planning process. Aligning these two processes would obviously be a great place to start in developing synergy around an institution's collective ambition.

West Chester University has a strategic plan page that features its plan—*Building on Excellence 2013-2022.* The plan itself begins with mission, vision, and values. It is comprehensive with the following sections: a process for engaging stakeholders, fiscal projections, a strategic planning model, goals and objectives, outcome measures, and a timeline. But an important part of developing constancy of purpose comes from another tab on the same page: *Middle States Accreditation 2011.* The timing is critical because it allows the "output" from accreditation to become the "input" to the strategic plan. Indeed, the accreditation section begins, "In June 2011, the Middle States Commission on Higher Education formally acted to reaffirm West Chester University's institutional accreditation, which is renewed every 10 years."

While the section goes on to state that the team's evaluation report highly praised WCU in several areas, it also adds, "The self-study serves as an important resource as West Chester University continues to move forward in developing and implementing the University's new strategic plan, *Building on Excellence*." The opportunities for improvement that flow from accreditation become the foundation for continuous improvement in this model. It is no accident that the next accreditation review is 2021 while the next comprehensive planning cycle begins in the following year. West Chester is following the recipe for "folding things in."

Don't Bury the Lead

As we have discussed, at the very center of *Future College* is the dynamic of structural tension. This requires that a desired state be significantly different from a current state which, in turn, causes a discrepancy that leads to structural tension. The forward movement in an institution occurs when individuals seek to resolve those differences through a bias for action.

An obvious problem occurs when the desired state is not distinctive, powerful, understood, and widely shared.

The evidence enumerated in Chapter Two, General Findings, unfortunately suggests that the problem is pervasive. That chapter asked the question, "What, if anything, does an institution's homepage reveal about its future?" The answer is very little. The overwhelming majority of information on institutions' homepages reflects the past (history, traditions, accomplishments) and the present (programs, campus tours, events). References to a desired state—in the form of a mission, vision, and values—were found by either clicking on an "About" tab, using the A-Z Index, or by means of the Search function. Even when using these discovery processes, only one in three institutions had all three elements that have been associated with a collective ambition.

All journalists are familiar with this concept—*burying the lead.* You have only a small amount of time to capture the attention of the continually-distracted reader. So, you want to take the essential points or facts of the story and present them at the very beginning.

Once you've hooked the reader on the lead, you have time to present the secondary materials in a deliberate way. You can fill in the rest. But if you aren't successful in making the case upfront about the importance of the story, there is a very good chance that he or she will move on to something that is more interesting or engaging.

The obvious change that should occur is to find ways to speak to an institution's collective ambition on its homepage. It can be done. A few institutions in this sample did it. Rice University has a very engaging website. It has "News at Rice," "Events at Rice," 'World Class Research," "Distinguished Academics," and a "Quick Facts" with a series of infographics:

- Consistently ranked among the top 29 universities in the U.S.
- 6-to-1 undergraduate student-to-faculty ratio with a median class size of 14
- 4,300 trees on our green campus located in the heart of the nation's fourth largest city
- Endowment asset per student: $867,770
- We meet 100% of demonstrated financial need of admitted students
- #4 values among private universities in the U.S.

But in the middle of all this is "Our Mission:"

As a leading research university with a distinctive commitment to undergraduate education, Rice University aspires to path breaking research, unsurpassed teaching and contributions to the betterment of our world. It seeks to fulfill this mission by cultivating a diverse community of learning and discovery that produces leaders across the spectrum of human endeavor.

Rice University really is a special place. Most research universities are much larger with much greater attention devoted to their graduate programs. Indeed, the standard rap against such institutions is that they devote too little attention to undergraduate teaching. But the very first phrase from above speaks to Rice's specialness. Indeed, Rice is a leading research university with almost $100 million in annual research but also 68 percent of Rice's undergraduates participate in research work during their time at Rice.

That is a mission-related lead story that shouldn't be buried. And Rice makes sure it isn't.

❖ ❖ ❖

There are many other ways to not bury the lead. Most of them do not involve the use of electronics. First, let's begin with story-telling. This was one of the stickiness evaluative criteria described in the Vision chapter. As the Heaths' state in *Made to Stick*:

"Stories have the amazing dual power to stimulate and to inspire. And most of the time we don't even have to use much creativity to harness these powers—we just need to be ready to spot the good ones that life generates every day."

Senior officials need to take the elements of the institution's mission, vision, and values that make it special and make them permanent talking points. The exercise is to continually scan the campus for stories that reflect "future college" and to weave them into speeches and presentations.

Then there is branding. This is the value of a having a simple, engaging, and distinctive vision statement: You can put it on the back of business cards and make posters for conference rooms. When problems occur that appear to be systemic in nature, check to see whether the breakdown is related to a violation of norms and then take appropriate action.

All of these are techniques associated with keeping the aspirations of a college or university where they need to be—that is, uppermost in the minds of all the stakeholders.

How are we Doing?

Ed Koch, the popular mayor of New York City through the 1980s, was famous for riding the subway, standing on street corners, and greeting people with the question, "How'm I doin'?" This final promising practice assumes that our institution has done everything right. It has dug deep into its history, traditions, and the current standards described by its accreditor to develop a strong mission statement that informs everyday decisions. It has created a compelling, shared vision that is distinctive and "sticks." It has produced a set of institutional values that are embraced as personal values and help to shape a strong culture.

But that is not enough. There still needs to be a feedback loop—a promising practice—that mimics Koch's famous question.

The reason goes back to Fritz's structural tension model. *Future College* is about a bias for action. That action results from the need for an institution to resolve the discrepancy between the desired state and the actual state. This usually takes place through the strategies and tactics associated with a comprehensive strategic plan.

The obvious follow-up question centers on success or failure—or "How are we doing?'

This sequence is at the heart of organizational learning and continuous improvement as described by every accrediting agency usually under an "institutional effectiveness" standard. For example, SACS has an institutional effectiveness standard (3.3):

The institution identifies expected outcomes, assesses the extent to which it achieves these outcomes, and provides evidence of improvement based on analysis of the results in each of the following areas: (Institutional Effectiveness) 3.3.1.1 educational programs, to include student learning outcomes 3.3.1.2 administrative support services 3.3.1.3 academic and student support services 3.3.1.4 research within its mission, if appropriate 3.3.1.5 community/public service within its mission, if appropriate.

This same approach is evident in the historic Shewhart Cycle of Plan-Do-Check-Act or its higher education equivalency of Plan-Do-Assess-Decide as described in general models of institutional effectiveness as described in *Noble Ambitions* (2013) and elsewhere.

The "evidence" or "check" or "assess" component provides the initial gap analysis. Some of our institutions described this component. Appalachian State University, as noted, has a strategic plan entitled *The Appalachian Experience: Envisioning a Just and Sustainable Future (2014-2019)* that begins with a Vision and Essential Character and Core Values followed by six Strategic Directions with a series of Initiatives each of which has a corresponding set of Metrics. These are the "How are we doing?" questions—the evidence or the check.

What happens when the assessment results show movement in the right direction? There should be increased energy, engagement, and self-efficacy. Individuals should be encouraged that the institution is making progress. But what happens when the results don't show any progress? Then what?

This is the "closing the loop" component because the individuals need to "decide" what to do next. The obvious approach is to change strategies, the resolution part of the structural tension model. This amounts to a course correction. It is saying, "We have the right future in mind but we are not taking the proper steps to get there." But there also needs to be some reflection on another question—"Do we have the right future?" The environment shifts. Many parts of the system can change. So, is our collective ambition still suitable? Do our purpose, vision, or beliefs need to be amended or adjusted to reflect this dynamism?

Some of the institutions in our sample, like Appalachian State, have aggressively designed this capability into creating their own future. Most do not.

This final promising practice is a fitting end to this book because it suggests the "end" is actually just the "beginning." *Future College* is not a destination, it is a journey. And like Alice, the question really is, "Which way do we go from here?" Unlike Alice (who responds by saying she didn't much care), we ought to care deeply about the answer. Because, as we have seen, if we don't provide the answer, others are prepared to provide the answer for us. That is simply abdicating the responsibility we have to our faculty, staff, students, and the larger society. So, in a high velocity environment it is critical that we are confident about our purpose and our beliefs, and that we constantly search the horizon for inspiration. It is also critical that we take stock of our progress and be willing to recalibrate along the way.

Check the map. Look out the window. And then enjoy the ride.

References

Chickering Art and Zelda Gamson, *7 Principles for Good Practice in Undergraduate Education*, (Racine, WI: The Johnson Foundation, 1989.

Clotfelter, Charles T., "Is Sports in Your Mission Statement?," *The Chronicle of Higher Education* (October 24, 2010).

Deal, Terrence E. and Allan A. Kennedy, *Corporate Cultures: The Rites and Rituals of Corporate Life*, (Cambridge, MA: Perseus Publishing), 2000.

Deming, W. Edwards, *Out of the Crisis* (Cambridge, MA: Massachusetts Institute of Technology of Technology Center for Advanced Engineering Study), 1982.

Deutcher, Irwin, *what we say/what we do,* (Glenville, IL: Scott, Foresman and Company), 1973.

Franklin, Benjamin, *The Means and Manner of Obtaining Virtue*, (New York, NY: Penguin Books), 1986.

Fritz, Robert, *The Path of Least Resistance for Managers* (San Francisco, CA: Berrett-Koehler Publishers), 1999.

Heath, Chip and Dan Heath, *Made to Stick: Why Some Ideas Survive and Others Die* (New York: Random House), 2007.

Kuh, George D. and Elizabeth J. Whitt, *The Invisible Tapestry: Culture in American Colleges and Universities.* ASHE-ERIC Higher Education Report No. 1. Washington, D.C.: Association for the Study of Higher Education, 1988.

Lencioni, Patrick, "Make Your Values Meaningful," *Harvard Business Review* (July, 2002).

Mourkogiannis, Nikos, *Purpose: The Starting Point of Great Companies* (New York: Palgrave Macmillan), 2006.

Quinn, Ryan W. and Robert E. Quinn, *Lift: Becoming a Positive Force in any Situation* (San Francisco, CA: Berrett-Koehler Publishers), 2009.

Ready, Douglas A. and Emily Truelove, "The Power of Collective Ambition," *Harvard Business Review* (December, 2011).

Schon, Donald, *Education the Reflective Practitioner: Toward a New Design for Teaching and Learning in the Professions* (San Francisco, CA: Jossey Bass), 1987.

Senge, Peter, *The Fifth Discipline* (New York, NY: Doubleday), 1990.

Senge, Peter, et al., *The Fifth Discipline Fieldbook* (New York, NY: Doubleday), 1994.

Seymour, Daniel, *Noble Ambitions: Mission, Vision, and Values in American Community Colleges* (Washington, DC: American Association of Community Colleges), 2013.

Seymour, Daniel, *Once Upon Campus: Lesson for Improving Quality and Productivity in Higher Education* (Washington, DC: American Council on Education), 1995.

Sinek, Simon, *Start with Why: How Great Leaders Inspire Everyone to Take Action* (New York, NY: Penguin Group), 2009.

'Survey of College and University Chief Academic Officers," *Inside Higher Ed*, 2015.

Weick, Karl, "Educational Organizations as Loosely Coupled Systems," *Administrative Science Quarterly*, 1976, 1-19.

Appendix A

Baccalaureate Colleges (Arts and Sciences)

Private 33		
Albion College	Gettysburg College	Lycoming College
Albright College	Goucher College	Monmouth College
Allegheny College	Grinnell College	Moravian College
Augustana College	Hartwick College	Oglethorpe University
Austin College	Juniata College	Pomona College
Beloit College	Kalamazoo College	Rhodes College
Bennington College	Kenyon College	Swarthmore College
Bowdoin College	Knox College	Union College
Bucknell University	Lake Forest College	University of Puget Sound
Carleton College	Lewis and Clark	Washington & Jeff. College
College of Wooster	Linfield College	Wofford College
Public 9		
Castleton State College	Louisiana State Univ.-Alexandra	SUNY-Purchase
Colorado Mesa University	Massachusetts College-Lib. Arts	Univ. of Wisconsin-Parkside
Fort Lewis College	New College of Florida	Western State Colorado Univ.

Research Universities (Very High Research Activity)

Public 24		
Colorado State University	University of Arkansas	University of Massachusetts
Georgia Tech University	University of Buffalo	University of Missouri
Indiana University	UC Berkeley	University of Oregon
Louisville University	UC Santa Barbara	University of Rochester
North Carolina State Univ.	UC Santa Cruz	University of South Florida
Oregon State University	University of Connecticut	University of Texas
Purdue University	University of Delaware	University of Utah
Stony Brook University	University of Kansas	University of Wisconsin-Mad.
Private 15		
Boston University	Dartmouth College	Rice University
Brandeis University	Emory University	Tufts University
Brown University	Johns Hopkins University	University of Miami
Carnegie Mellon University	Northwestern University	University of Pennsylvania
Columbia University	Rensselaer Polytechnic Univ.	University of Southern Cal.

Master's Colleges & Universities (Larger Programs)

Public 36		
Appalachian State University	James Madison University	Slippery Rock University
Austin Peay State University	Kean University	Southern Utah University
Bloomsburg Univ. of Penn	Kutztown University	SUNY, New Paltz
Cal. State University, Chico	Marshall University	Texas State University
Cal. State, East Bay	McNeese State University	Towson University
Cal. State, Sacramento	Montclair State University	Univ. of Central Oklahoma
Central Conn. State Univ.	Morehead State University	University of Northern Iowa
Eastern Michigan University	NW Missouri State Univ.	Wayne State University

Emporia State University	Plymouth State University	West Chester University
Framingham State University	Rhode Island College	Western Washington Univ.
Frostburg State University	San Francisco State University	Winthrop University
Governors State University	St. Cloud State University	Youngstown State University
Private 24		
Alfred University	Monmouth University	Springfield College
Bentley University	Pacific University	Stetson University
Chapman University	Quinnipiac University	University of Bridgeport
Drake University	Rider University	University of Findlay
Emerson University	Robert Morris University	University of New England
Ithaca College	Rochester Institute of Tech.	University of Redlands
Johnson and Wales University	Rollins College	Webster University
Lesley University	Roosevelt University	Wilkes University

Appendix B

Middle States Commission on Higher Education (MSCHE)

The most recent MSCHE standards (2015) were developed through a comprehensive process lasting nearly 18 months. The Steering Committee followed a set of Guiding Principles. The four Guiding Principles were developed by the Commission to reflect the areas that were identified as the most important to the membership of the Commission: Mission-Centric Quality Assurance, the Student Learning Experience, Continuous Improvement, and Supporting Innovation.

There are seven Standards: Mission and Goals; Ethics and Integrity; Design and Delivery of the Student Learning Experience; Support of the Student Experience; Educational Effectiveness Assessment; Planning, Resources, and Institutional Improvement; and Governance, Leadership, and Administration.

Standard 1 (Mission and Goals) begins with the following statement:

> The institution's mission defines its purpose within the context of higher education, the students it serves, and what it intends to accomplish. The institution's stated goals are clearly linked to its mission and specify how the institution fulfills its mission.

There are four Criteria associated with this initial Standard:

1. clearly defined mission and goals that:
   a. are developed through appropriate collaborative participation by all who facilitate or are otherwise responsible for institutional development and improvement;
   b. address external as well as internal contexts and constituencies;
   c. are approved and supported by the governing body;
   d. guide faculty, administration, staff, and governing structures in making decisions related to planning, resource allocation, program and curricular development, and the definition of institutional and educational outcomes;
   e. include support of scholarly inquiry and creative activity, at levels and of the type appropriate to the institution;
   f. are publicized and widely known by the institution's internal stakeholders;
   g. are periodically evaluated;
2. institutional goals that are realistic, appropriate to higher education, and consistent with mission;
3. goals that focus on student learning and related outcomes and on institutional improvement; are supported by administrative, educational, and student support programs and services; and are consistent with institutional mission; and
4. periodic assessment of mission and goals to ensure they are relevant and achievable.

Importantly, most of the other MSCHE Standards reference Standard I on Mission and Goals in their introduction:

- Standard II (Ethics and Integrity—In all activities, whether internal or external, an institution must be faithful to its mission, honor its contracts and commitments, adhere to its policies, and represent itself truthfully.
- Standard IV (Support of the Student Experience)—Across all educational experiences, settings, levels, and instructional modalities, the institution recruits and admits students whose interests, abilities, experiences, and goals are congruent with its mission and educational offerings.

- Standard V (Educational Effectiveness Assessment)—Assessment of student learning and achievement demonstrates that the institution's students have accomplished educational goals consistent with their program of study, degree level, the institution's mission, and appropriate expectations for institutions of higher education.
- Standard VI (Planning, Resources, and Institutional Improvement)—The institution's planning processes, resources, and structures are aligned with each other and are sufficient to fulfill its mission and goals, to continuously assess and improve its programs and services, and to respond effectively to opportunities and challenges.
- Standard VII (Governance, Leadership, and Administration)— The institution is governed and administered in a manner that allows it to realize its stated mission and goals in a way that effectively benefits the institution, its students, and the other constituencies it serves.

New England Association of Schools and Colleges (NEASC)

The 11 Standards of NEASC were adopted in 2011. The Preamble to the Standards includes the following global statement that relates to mission:

Each of the eleven Standards articulates a dimension of institutional quality. In applying the Standards, the Commission assesses and makes a determination about the effectiveness of the institution as a whole. The institution that meets the Standards:

- has clearly defined purposes appropriate to an institution of higher learning;
- has assembled and organized those resources necessary to achieve its purposes;
- is achieving its purposes;
- has the ability to continue to achieve its purposes.

The first Standard is Mission and Purposes. The introduction to the Standard follows:

> The institution's mission and purposes are appropriate to higher education, consistent with its charter or other operating authority, and implemented in a manner that complies with the Standards of the Commission on

Institutions of Higher Education. The institution's mission gives direction to its activities and provides a basis for the assessment and enhancement of the institution's effectiveness.

1.1 The mission of the institution defines its distinctive character, addresses the needs of society and identifies the students the institution seeks to serve, and reflects both the institution's traditions and its vision for the future. The institution's mission provides the basis upon which the institution identifies its priorities, plans its future and evaluates its endeavors; it provides a basis for the evaluation of the institution against the Commission's Standards.

1.2 The institution's mission is set forth in a concise statement that is formally adopted by the governing board and appears in appropriate institutional publications.

1.3 The institution's purposes are concrete and realistic and further define its educational and other dimensions, including scholarship, research, and public service. Consistent with its mission, the institution endeavors to enhance the communities it serves.

1.4 The mission and purposes of the institution are accepted and widely understood by its governing board, administration, faculty, staff, and students. They provide direction to the curricula and other activities and form the basis on which expectations for student learning are developed. Specific objectives, reflective of the institution's overall mission and purposes, are developed by the institution's individual units.

1.5 The institution periodically re-evaluates the content and pertinence of its mission and purposes, assessing their usefulness in providing overall direction in planning and resource allocation. The results of this evaluation are used to enhance institutional effectiveness.

In addition, elements of the institution's mission and purpose are discussed in many of the other Standards.

Standard Two: Planning and Evaluation

> The institution undertakes planning and evaluation to accomplish and improve the achievement of its mission and purposes. It identifies its planning and evaluation priorities and pursues them effectively.

Standard Three: Organization and Governance

> The institution has a system of governance that facilitates the accomplishment of its mission and purposes and supports institutional effectiveness and integrity.

Standard Four: The Academic Program

> The institution's academic programs are consistent with and serve to fulfill its mission and purposes.

Standard Five: Faculty

> The institution develops a faculty that is suited to the fulfillment of the institution's mission. Faculty qualifications, numbers, and performance are sufficient to accomplish the institution's mission and purposes.

Standard Six: Students

> Consistent with its mission, the institution defines the characteristics of the students it seeks to serve and provides an environment that fosters the intellectual and personal development of its students.

Standard Seven: Library and Other Information Resources

> The institution provides sufficient and appropriate library and information resources. The institution provides adequate access to these resources and demonstrates their effectiveness in fulfilling its mission.

Standard Eight: Physical and Technological Resources

> The institution has sufficient and appropriate physical and technological resources necessary for the achievement of its purposes. It manages and maintains these resources in a manner to sustain and enhance the realization of institutional purposes.

Standard Eleven: Integrity

> Through its policies and practices, the institution endeavors to exemplify the values it articulates in its mission and related statements.

Northwest Commission on Colleges and Universities (NWCCU)

The five NWCCU Standards for Accreditation were revised in 2010 and are best understood within the context of a seven-year accreditation cycle. The Standards are interconnected and build upon each other in a recursive cycle of continuous improvement.

Standard One is "Mission, Core Themes, and Expectations" and begins:

> The institution articulates its purpose in a mission statement, and identifies core themes that comprise essential elements of that mission. In an examination of its purpose, characteristics, and expectations, the institution defines the parameters for mission fulfillment. Guided by that definition, it identifies an acceptable threshold or extent of mission fulfillment

The Standard goes on to enumerate two components: Mission and Core Themes.

1.A Mission

1.A.1 The institution has a widely published mission statement—approved by its governing board—that articulates a purpose appropriate for an institution of higher learning, gives direction for its efforts, and derives from, and is generally understood by, its community.

1.A.2 The institution defines mission fulfillment in the context of its purpose, characteristics, and expectations. Guided by that definition, it articulates institutional accomplishments or outcomes that represent an acceptable threshold or extent of mission fulfillment.

1.B Core Themes

1.B.1 The institution identifies core themes that individually manifest essential elements of its mission and collectively encompass its mission.

1.B.2 The institution establishes objectives for each of its core themes and identifies meaningful, assessable, and verifiable indicators of achievement that form the basis for evaluating accomplishment of the objectives of its core themes.

Other Standards have mission-related language that aligns with the Mission and Core Themes described in Standard One:

Standard Two (Resources and Capacity): By documenting the adequacy of its resources and capacity, the institution demonstrates the potential to fulfill its mission, accomplish its core theme objectives, and achieve the intended outcomes of its programs and services, wherever offered and however delivered.

> Standard Three (Planning and Implementation): The institution engages in ongoing, participatory planning that provides direction for the institution and leads to the achievement of the intended outcomes of its programs and services, accomplishment of its core themes, and fulfillment of its mission.

Most importantly, Standard Five is explicit about its role in relation to Mission. "Mission Fulfillment, Adaptation, and Sustainability" contains the following introductory language:

> Based on its definition of mission fulfillment and informed by the results of its analysis of accomplishment of its core theme objectives, the institution develops and publishes evidence-based evaluations regarding the extent to which it is fulfilling its mission. The institution regularly monitors its internal and external environments to determine how and to what degree changing circumstances may impact its mission and its ability to fulfill that mission. It demonstrates that it is capable of adapting, when necessary, its mission, core themes, programs, and services to accommodate changing and emerging needs, trends, and influences to ensure enduring institutional relevancy, productivity, viability, and sustainability.

The first element of this final Standard tends to serve as a bookend to Standard One "Mission, Core Themes, and Expectations" and starts with the following language:

> 5.A Mission Fulfillment
>
> 5.A.1 The institution engages in regular, systematic, participatory, self-reflective, and evidence-based assessment of its accomplishments.
>
> 5.A.2 Based on its definition of mission fulfillment, the institution uses assessment results to make determinations of quality, effectiveness, and mission fulfillment and communicates its conclusions to appropriate constituencies and the public.

North Central Association Higher Learning Commission (NCAHLC)

The NCAHLC has five criteria (effective 2013) beginning with the Criterion One (Mission):

> The institution's mission is clear and articulated publicly;
> it guides the institution's operations

There are a series of Core Components associated with Criterion One:

1.A. The institution's mission is broadly understood within the institution and guides its operations.

1. The mission statement is developed through a process suited to the nature and culture of the institution and is adopted by the governing board.
2. The institution's academic programs, student support services, and enrollment profile are consistent with its stated mission.
3. The institution's planning and budgeting priorities align with and support the mission. (This sub-component may be addressed by reference to the response to Criterion 5.C.1.)

1.B. The mission is articulated publicly.

1. The institution clearly articulates its mission through one or more public documents, such as statements of purpose, vision, values, goals, plans, or institutional priorities.
2. The mission document or documents are current and explain the extent of the institution's emphasis on the various aspects of its mission, such as instruction, scholarship, research, application of research, creative works, clinical service, public service, economic development, and religious or cultural purpose.

3. The mission document or documents identify the nature, scope, and intended constituents of the higher education programs and services the institution provides.

1.C. The institution understands the relationship between its mission and the diversity of society.

1. The institution addresses its role in a multicultural society.
2. The institution's processes and activities reflect attention to human diversity as appropriate within its mission and for the constituencies it serves.

1.D. The institution's mission demonstrates commitment to the public good.

1. Actions and decisions reflect an understanding that in its educational role the institution serves the public, not solely the institution, and thus entails a public obligation.
2. The institution's educational responsibilities take primacy over other purposes, such as generating financial returns for investors, contributing to a related or parent organization, or supporting external interests.
3. The institution engages with its identified external constituencies and communities of interest and responds to their needs as its mission and capacity allow.

Criterion Five (Resources, Planning, and Institutional Effectiveness) begins with following statement:

> The institution's resources, structures, and processes are sufficient to fulfill its mission, improve the quality of its educational offerings, and respond to future challenges and opportunities. The institution plans for the future.

Throughout this final section there are specific references to the link between mission and resource, planning, and institutional elements. For example:

> 5A3 The goals incorporated into mission statements or elaborations of mission statements are realistic in light of the institution's organization, resources, and opportunities.
>
> 5B The institution's governance and administrative structures promote effective leadership and support collaborative processes that enable the institution to fulfill its mission.
>
> 5C1 The institution allocates its resources in alignment with its mission and priorities.

Southern Association of Colleges and Schools (SACS)

The Principles of Accreditation for SACS that were adopted in 2013 is divided into two main categories: Core Requirements and Comprehensive Standards. The Core Requirements are basic, broad-based foundational requirements that an institution must meet, one of which is Institutional Mission:

> The institution has a clearly defined, comprehensive, and published mission statement that is specific to the institution and appropriate for higher education. The mission addresses teaching and learning and, where applicable, research and public service.

Institutional Mission is also embedded in the idea of Institutional Effectiveness which is another one of the Core Requirements:

> The institution engages in ongoing, integrated, and institution-wide research-based planning and evaluation processes that (1) incorporate a systematic review of institutional mission, goals, and outcomes; (2) result in continuing improvement in institutional quality; and (3) demonstrate the institution is effectively accomplishing its mission.

The Comprehensive Standards set forth requirements in four areas: institutional mission, governance, and effectiveness; programs; resources; and institutional responsibility for Commission policies.

The Institutional Mission standard states:

> The mission statement is current and comprehensive, accurately guides the institution's operations, is periodically reviewed and updated, is approved by the governing board, and is communicated to the institution's constituencies. (Mission)

There is also an Institutional Effectiveness area which involves the following: '

> The institution identifies expected outcomes, assesses the extent to which it achieves these outcomes, and provides evidence of improvement based on analysis of the results in each of the following areas: educational programs, to include student learning outcomes; administrative support services; academic and student support services; research within its mission, if appropriate; and community/public service within its mission, if appropriate.

Western Association of Schools and Colleges (WASC)

WASC is divided into two divisions: Junior Colleges and Senior Colleges and Universities. The 2013 *Handbook of Accreditation* for the Senior Colleges and Universities consists of four standards. The first is Defining Institutional Purposes/Ensuring Educational Objectives.

The institution defines its purposes and establishes educational objectives aligned with those purposes. The institution has a clear and explicit sense of its essential values and character, its distinctive elements, its place in both the higher education community and society, and its contribution to the public good. It functions with integrity, transparency, and autonomy.

Under the heading of Institutional Purposes are the following criteria:

1.1 The institution's formally approved statements of purpose are appropriate for an institution of higher education and clearly define its essential values and character and ways in which it contributes to the public good.

Guidelines: The institution has a published mission statement that clearly describes its purposes. The institution's purposes fall within recognized academic areas and/or disciplines.

1.2 Educational objectives are widely recognized throughout the institution, are consistent with stated purposes, and are demonstrably achieved. The institution regularly generates, evaluates, and makes public data about student achievement, including measures of retention and graduation, and evidence of student learning.

1.3 The institution publicly states its commitment to academic freedom for faculty, staff, and students, and acts accordingly. This commitment affirms that those in the academy are free to share their convictions and responsible conclusions with their colleagues and students in their teaching and writing.

Guidelines: The institution has published or has readily available policies on academic freedom. For those institutions that strive to instill specific beliefs and world views, policies clearly state how these views are implemented and ensure that these conditions are consistent with generally recognized principles of academic freedom. Due-process procedures are disseminated, demonstrating that faculty and students are protected in their quest for truth.

1.4 Consistent with its purposes and character, the institution demonstrates an appropriate response to the increasing diversity in society through its policies, its educational and co-curricular programs, its hiring and admissions criteria, and its administrative and organizational practices.

Guidelines: The institution has demonstrated institutional commitment to the principles enunciated in the WSCUC Diversity Policy.

Institutional Purpose also appears in other WSCUC Standards:

Standard 2: Achieving Educational Objectives Through Core Functions

The institution achieves its purposes and attains its educational objectives at the institutional and program level through the core functions of teaching and learning, scholarship and creative activity, and support for student learning and success.

Standard 3: Developing and Applying Resources and Organizational Structures to Ensure Quality and Sustainability

The institution sustains its operations and supports the achievement of its educational objectives through investments in human, physical, fiscal, technological, and information resources and through an appropriate and effective set of organizational and decision-making structures. These key resources and organizational structures promote the achievement of institutional purposes and educational objectives and create a high-quality environment for learning.

Standard 4: Creating an Organization Committed to Quality Assurance, Institutional Learning, and Improvement

The institution engages in sustained, evidence-based, and participatory self-reflection about how effectively it is accomplishing its purposes and achieving its educational objectives. The institution considers the changing environment of higher education in envisioning its future. These activities inform both institutional planning and systematic evaluations of educational effectiveness. The results of institutional inquiry, research, and data collection are used to establish priorities, to plan, and to improve quality and effectiveness.

Made in the USA
Columbia, SC
16 June 2018